Original Title: Cyprus Tax Solution.

©Cyprus Tax Solution, Víctor Martínez and Carlos Martínez, 2024.

Authors: Víctor Martínez and Carlos Martínez.

© Cover and illustrations: Víctor Martínez and Carlos Martínez.

Layout and design: Víctor Martínez and Carlos Martínez.

All rights reserved.

This publication may not be reproduced, stored, recorded, or transmitted, in whole or in part, in any form or by any means—mechanical, photochemical, electronic, magnetic, electro-optical, including photocopying and information retrieval systems, or any other present or future method—without the prior written permission of the copyright holders.

CYPRUS TAX SOLUTION

Essential guide for personal and business relocation to Cyprus.

INDEX

1. Introduction.
2. Our Personal Experience.
3. Purpose of Our Work and Contact.
4. Interesting Professions for Relocating to Cyprus.
5. Corporate Migration.
6. Business Formation.
7. Yellow Slip.
8. Non-domicile.
9. Procedure: If You Are Not a Citizen of the European Union.
10. Company VAT Registration + Company Tax Registration + Company Management Registration.
11. Personal Tax Registration.
12. Intra-community or Cross-border VAT (VIES).
13. Salary.
14. IP Box.
15. Accounting.
16. Investment: Cryptocurrencies, ETFs, Trading, Stock Market...
17. Bank Accounts.
18. Real Estate: Rental and Purchase of Housing.
19. Registering Electricity Supply.
20. Registering Water Supply.
21. Insurance: Health and Vehicle.
22. Rental and Purchase of Vehicles.
23. Companies: Internet and Telephone.
24. Coworking Spaces.
25. Home Delivery Food.
26. Nationality.
27. Security.
28. Schooling.
29. Frequently Asked Questions.
30. History of Cyprus.
31. Cypriot Banking Crisis.
32. Major Cities and Tourist Sites.
33. Traditional Food.
34. Fun Facts.

1
INTRODUCTION.

In the heart of the Mediterranean, Cyprus emerges not only as a crossroad of cultures and a touristic gem but also as an attractive hub for individuals and businesses seeking to optimize their tax landscape and leverage a favorable business environment.

This book, the result of accumulated experience and deep knowledge from a team of specialist advisors, is proposed as an essential guide for those considering changing their tax residence to Cyprus, for both individuals and corporate entities.

Through its pages, we will share our personal experience, not just as advisors but as active participants in the process of transitioning to a new tax residence in Cyprus.

Our purpose extends beyond mere consultancy; we aim to be a bridge that connects dreams with realities, facilitating a smooth change in compliance with legal regulations.

Our clients span a wide spectrum, from individual entrepreneurs to multinational corporations, including those seeking a safe haven for their investments in cryptocurrencies, ETFs, trading, and the stock market.

For each, Cyprus offers fertile ground for prosperity and growth.

From corporate migration and business creation to obtaining the "Yellow Slip," acquiring "non-domicile" status, and handling specific aspects, this book covers all the necessary details for a successful transition.

We detail the procedures for VAT registration and business management, as well as for obtaining tax benefits through the "IP Box," and we address the specifics of accounting in the Cypriot context.

Investment, buying or renting vehicles, managing bank accounts, the real estate market, and even such everyday but crucial aspects as insurance and schooling, are clarified in detail, providing a compendium of essential knowledge for the modern expatriate.

Furthermore, due to the importance of integrating into the rich Cypriot culture, we discuss aspects such as safety and explore the major cities and tourist sites, not forgetting to indulge in its traditional food.

This book is not only a tax and business guide but also a window into life in Cyprus, offering answers to frequently asked questions and clearing the path towards acquiring a new nationality, if needed.

Welcome to the next chapter of your life in Cyprus, where history, innovation, and opportunity meet to create a very prosperous future.

2

OUR PERSONAL EXPERIENCE.

In the search for new horizons that combined security, favorable taxation, and a stable environment for living and doing business, we, initially two Spanish entrepreneurs with solid experience in consulting and insurance, as well as entrepreneurship through selling products on Amazon globally, made the decision to leave behind our beloved country, Spain.

Despite the deep love we felt for every corner of our land and the warmth of its people, the challenges of high taxes, increasing insecurity in the streets, and political instability compelled us to seek an alternative that aligned more closely with our personal and professional aspirations.

After an exhaustive analysis of various options, such as Portugal, Malta, Estonia, Andorra, Bulgaria, and Hungary, Cyprus emerged as the ideal destination.

The Mediterranean island promised not only a safe environment and an attractive tax structure but also the opportunity to immerse ourselves in a rich culture and enjoy an enviable lifestyle. However, the transition was not simple.

Closing economic activity in Spain involved facing a series of challenges, although it is worth noting that the most annoying was the continuous disappointment we received from consultants who, in theory, were specialized in company formation in Cyprus, and did not remotely meet expectations in terms of efficiency, commitment, and professionalism.

Despite the poor management by the "expert" advisors we hired, we did not give up, and our determination led us to personally tackle the cumbersome bureaucracy in Cyprus.

This learning process, although arduous, allowed us to acquire a deep understanding of the necessary procedures for establishing and transferring economic activity to Cyprus in an optimized and professional manner.

The experience was not only transformative on a personal and professional level but also planted the seed for a new venture.

Once settled in Cyprus, and after experiencing firsthand the benefits of our decision, we began to share our newly acquired knowledge and experiences with friends, industry colleagues, and other professionals.

The help proved invaluable for many who were looking to improve their tax situation and find a balance between work and personal life in a more favorable environment.

The demand for advice grew to such an extent that we were compelled to formalize our offering, transforming the experiences, lessons learned, and contacts made into a professional service for those interested in relocating to Cyprus.

Today, we offer a unique service, characterized by ongoing support and high-quality advice, specializing in the creation of international companies in Cyprus.

Our personalized approach, based on our own journey and overcome challenges, allows us to guide clients through the bureaucratic maze, ensuring a 100% successful relocation and establishment on the island.

Through consultancy, we have managed to build a bridge between our Spanish roots and our adopted Cypriot homeland, demonstrating that it is possible to reinvent oneself and thrive in a new environment, without forgetting where we come from.

3

PURPOSE OF OUR WORK AND CONTACT

Cyprus Tax Solution specializes in offering strategic and personalized tax solutions, with the primary objective of optimizing your tax situation in Cyprus.

We strive to ensure that, within the legal framework, you pay the minimum possible in taxes, thus maximizing your benefits and operational efficiency.

We understand that every company has unique needs, so our proposal is always personalized. However, for most of our clients, we have found one particularly effective structure.

This strategic structure allows optimal leverage of the country's favorable tax regime.

Therefore, your company can benefit from a corporate tax rate as low as 12.50% annually.

Additionally, we will manage the registration in the Cyprus "Non-Dom" regime, which means that the applicable taxes on dividend payments to your physical person would be reduced to 2.65% annually for a period of 17 years, in accordance with an agreement with the Cypriot public administration.

This approach is not only efficient but also fully legal under the current tax legislation in Cyprus.

This regime offers a significant tax advantage without compromising the legality or transparency of your financial operations.

A notable aspect of this regime is the flexibility it offers in terms of residency.

To achieve these tax advantages, you are required to reside in Cyprus for only 60 days a year, which provides great freedom to manage your time and physical presence.

It is important, however, to ensure that you do not spend more than 183 days in another country, so as not to affect your tax status in Cyprus.

Finally, within this tax scheme, you will also have the option to receive a monthly salary exempt from self-employment contributions and personal income tax (IRPF).

Instead of traditional social security contributions, you can opt to purchase private health insurance, which is a condition to enjoy this benefit.

Our team of experts is dedicated to guiding you through every step of this process, ensuring that every aspect of the tax structure is handled with professionalism, precision, and in line with your business and personal objectives.

With our advice, you can trust that your tax situation will not only be optimized but also sustainable in the long term.

We are endorsed by hundreds of clients, mostly from Spain, Germany, France, and Italy, who have already realized their dreams with our tax optimization, transparency, legality, and quality personalized service.

If you want to create your company in Cyprus or need personalized advice to deeply understand your tax situation, contact us through:

-**Website:** www.solucionfiscalchipre.com
-**Email:** cyprustaxsolution@gmail.com
-**Mobile phone with WhatsApp:** +357 99953934

4

INTERESTING PROFESSIONS FOR MOVING TO CYPRUS.

We manage a wide variety of clients engaged in different economic activities across many European Union countries.

However, digital nomads who benefit from the freedom to work from anywhere make up approximately 70% of our clients who decide to establish their company in Cyprus and live there for at least 60 days a year.

This is due to the flexibility they have, which allows them to explore new cultures and lifestyles without compromising their careers or income.

Consequently, Cyprus, with its pleasant climate, rich cultural history, and favorable tax regime for many types of foreign workers and companies, has become an attractive destination for them.

Some of our clients who are digital nomads engage in the following activities:

-Software development and web design.
-Digital marketing and social media management.
-Content creation on websites like YouTube, social media platforms, as well as blogging and online course creation.
-Consulting in finance, education, therapies, and online coaching.
-E-commerce through selling products globally on platforms like Amazon, online stores, and dropshipping.
-Graphic design and animation.
-Programming and data analysis.
-Virtual assistant services.
-Online investment and trading.
-Video game development.
-Music production and sound engineering.
-Virtual architecture and interior design.
-Cybersecurity and IT consulting.

5

CORPORATE MIGRATION

Planning corporate migration while considering the fiscal year of the involved jurisdictions is essential to ensure a smooth and efficient transition for businesses seeking to relocate or expand internationally.

This approach not only facilitates administrative management but is also key to optimizing the overall tax burden.

Below, we delve into the importance of this planning and offer practical considerations for its implementation, with a special focus on migration during the first 6 months of the year to avoid double taxation.

Importance of planning according to the fiscal year:

-Fiscal year of each country: It is crucial to know the fiscal year of both the originating and destination jurisdictions. For example, the fiscal year in Spain runs from January 1 to December 31, while in other countries it may vary. Cyprus, on the other hand, also follows the calendar year for tax purposes.

-Fiscal clarity: Starting operations in a new country at the beginning of its fiscal year provides a clear basis for accounting and tax reporting, aligning business activities with the complete fiscal cycle of the destination country.

-Avoiding double taxation: Planning migration in accordance with fiscal years allows companies to significantly reduce the risk of being taxed twice on the same income. Migrating during the first 6 months of the fiscal year can be particularly strategic, as it allows the company to establish its new tax home before the fiscal year's midpoint, leveraging double taxation treaties to properly allocate the current year's income.

- **Cash flow and budgeting:** Understanding and planning according to the fiscal cycle facilitates better cash flow management and budgeting, taking into account tax and financial obligations in both jurisdictions.

- **Regulatory compliance:** Aligning with the fiscal calendar ensures effective adherence to regulatory and reporting requirements, simplifying compliance across multiple jurisdictions.

- **Professional consultancy:** Given the complexity of international tax laws and the potential for legislative changes, the guidance of a tax expert is invaluable. An advisor can determine the optimal timing for migration, maximizing tax benefits and mitigating risks.

- **Documentation preparation and compliance:** Anticipating documentation preparation and understanding compliance requirements are essential to facilitating an efficient transition and avoiding tax issues. Therefore, we recommend initiating the creation of the new company in Cyprus 1-2 months in advance.

- **Processing modelo 030 in Spain:** This form corresponds to the Census of Taxpayers—Census Declaration for registration, change of address, and/or change of personal data. Its submission is not mandatory but advisable. Regarding the income for the year in which you change your residence from your country to Cyprus, if you do not submit the Modelo 030, you will need to demonstrate and provide necessary documentation that you have not been a tax resident in Spain or your country for more than 183 days and, therefore, are not obligated to file that year's income tax.

- **Registration at your country's embassy in Cyprus:**
This is not mandatory but advisable to continue the process of disassociating from your country of origin.
The documents required for registration are:

- Yellow slip + 1 photocopy
- 1 passport-sized photo
- National ID + Passport + 1 photocopy of each document.

6

COMPANY FORMATION.

Benefits: Corporate Tax 12.5%

Approximate duration: From 3 weeks to 1 month.

Information needed for processing:

-3 possible names for the company written in order of preference.

If you want to expedite the process, which typically takes about 7-14 days, you can indicate this, and we will show you various names that the consultancy has purchased.

You can choose one of these, and we can transfer it to you.

-Paragraph description of the business in English.

-Photos of ID and passport.

-Name of the company director (there can be 2 partners as directors).

-Name of the company secretary (there can be only 1 secretary).

-If there are multiple partners-shareholders, the percentage of shares each one holds in the new company must be determined.

7

YELLOW SLIP

The "Yellow Slip" is an official document known as the Permanent Residence Registration Certificate for European Union Citizens.

This document is issued to citizens of the European Union (EU) and their family members who reside in Cyprus for a period of at least two months per year.

The "Yellow Slip" is yellow in color, hence its informal name, and serves as proof of legal residence in Cyprus for EU citizens and their direct relatives.

It allows holders to access a range of rights and services in Cyprus, such as public healthcare, public education, and employment.

Once the company is established, we can process the Yellow Slips.

It is a procedure in which you must go in person to the immigration office in Nicosia (Cyprus), and you will be accompanied by an employee from the consultancy who will guide and assist you throughout.

You will be notified when you have the appointment, and with your acceptance, the day and time will be confirmed for you to attend in person.

Necessary information for processing:

-3 months of bank statements from your personal account: It is recommended to show a minimum monthly income of €1500.

-3 receipts of purchases made in Cyprus and the corresponding bank statement: Examples include supermarket, coffee shop, bar food, taxi, ...

-Copy of Passport.

-Proof of salary income: 3 bank statements showing salary deposits or a work contract.

-Health insurance: If the client does not have one, the advisory service will help arrange it for approximately €200, which includes the minimum coverage required for validation. In addition to the contract documentation, the conditions of the insurance showing the coverage must be provided.

-Phone number: It can be from your country of origin or from Cyprus if you have one.

-1-year rental contract for the residence in Cyprus.

8

NON-DOMICILE

It is a special tax regime that allows those who are not tax residents of Cyprus to enjoy significant tax benefits.

Under this regime, individuals who are considered "non-domiciled" in Cyprus can reduce taxes on foreign income (all income that comes from outside Cyprus).

Once the Yellow Slip is processed, we can apply for Non-Domicile status.

You will receive the Non-Domicile permit approximately at the beginning of the following year.

The tax authorities will check if you have stayed in Cyprus for 60 days and not more than 183 days in any other country.

Additionally, they will request bank statements for the entire year and an Excel analysis of all your travels around the world with boarding passes.

Benefits:

-Dividend payments are taxed at 2.65% up to €180,000. Any amount exceeding €180,000 is taxed at 0%.

-A contract is established with the Cypriot government that maintains these conditions for 17 years.

-You only need to live in Cyprus for 60 days to obtain residency and tax benefits.

Important considerations:

If you live in Cyprus and consider yourself a tax resident of that country, you must be careful not to spend more than 183 days in Spain for several reasons:

-Tax residency status: Spending more than 183 days in Spain automatically makes you a Spanish tax resident according to Spanish law. This means that your global income would be subject to taxation in Spain. As a Spanish tax resident, you must declare and pay taxes not only on income generated in Spain but also on any income earned in other countries, including Cyprus.

-Double taxation: Although Spain and other European Union countries have a double taxation treaty with Cyprus to prevent their citizens from paying taxes twice on the same income, managing these tax credits can be complex and does not necessarily eliminate the tax burden entirely. You might find yourself in a situation where you need to file tax returns in both countries and navigate the process of claiming tax credits for taxes paid in the other country, which can be complicated and could result in higher tax payments than expected.

-Additional criteria: Spain and other EU countries consider additional factors to determine tax residency, such as the center of economic interests, the location of your spouse and children, and whether you have a permanent home available in your country of origin (whether rented or owned). This means that even if you spend less than 183 days in Spain, you could still be considered a tax resident if the government can prove that your economic or personal ties are stronger with your country of origin than with any other country. Therefore, you should not have economic or family interests in your country of origin, and you should not have a rented property or, if you own it, you should rent it out to third parties.

-Avoiding double taxation: To avoid becoming a tax resident in both countries and facing double taxation, it is important to carefully plan your stays in your home country and Cyprus. Keeping a detailed record of your presence in each country and seeking professional tax advice is essential.

Information required for processing:

-Photo of Yellow Slips.

-Identification (ID card) and passport of your parents.

-Your birth certificate.

-Original rental contract for housing in Cyprus:
It must be sent by regular mail to the central offices or handed to the consultancy employee in person when you personally go to Nicosia to process the Yellow Slips.

-Flight documents: Invoice, flight booking, airport boarding pass.

Important notice: The boarding pass is a very important document. Whenever you travel to another country, you must keep the boarding document, as the public administration of Cyprus may request it at the end of the year to verify that you have been in the country for at least 60 days.

9

PROCEDURE:
NON-EUROPEAN UNION CITIZEN.

All individuals who are not citizens of the European Union and wish to establish their company in Cyprus and obtain tax residency must process either "Temporary Residence" or "Permanent Residence."

Temporary residence.

The temporary residence permit in Cyprus, commonly known as the Pink Slip, allows non-European Union passport holders to extend their stay in Cyprus for more than 3 months (90 days). It also allows tourists and visitors to extend their stay regardless of the duration of their initial visa.
They must apply before their current visa expires.

Benefits:

- It can extend the stay in Cyprus for non-Europeans up to a year without the need for a visa.
- It is renewable.
- Families can apply simultaneously; each family member submits a separate application form and obtains temporary residence.

Requirements:

- Rent a house or apartment in Cyprus for one year.
- Need to prove an adequate amount exceeding €5,000 per individual.

-To process the children's applications, it must be proven that the parents are married.

Restrictions:

-The applicant must stay in Cyprus for at least a total of 90 days within one full year, but this time does not need to be consecutive. Additionally, they can travel to any other country they wish for approximately 9 months but cannot stay in the same place for more than 3 months. The only country where they can stay for the entire year or more than 3 consecutive months per year is Cyprus.
-There is no right to work in Cyprus.
-It is granted only to non-EU citizens who wish to extend their stay in Cyprus.
-Valid for one year, renewable annually.

Documents:

-Application form for temporary residence in Cyprus.
-One-year rental contract or sale contract for a house or apartment.
-Health insurance.
-Copy of the passport.
-Copy of the passport or other travel document, indicating the most recent arrival in the Republic of Cyprus and the corresponding visa.
-Copy of the marriage certificate, duly certified and translated.
-Certified and translated birth certificates of the children.
-Original criminal record certificate.
-Original medical analyses (Hepatitis B and C, HIV, syphilis, as well as a chest X-ray for tuberculosis with a doctor's opinion, sealed by a specialist doctor from the Republic of Cyprus).

- Bank statement from a foreign bank account showing an adequate amount of funds or stable income derived from various sources such as pension, dividends, salary outside Cyprus, deposit interest, etc.
- Certificate from a Cypriot banking institution or bank statement showing transfers from abroad to this entity for a minimum value of €5,000 per person applying for temporary residence.
- Original bank guarantee letter issued by a bank in Cyprus. (A deposit must be left with the bank while the temporary residence is maintained).

The processing time for the bank to issue the bank guarantees is 1 to 2 days.

Deposits:
    1. Eastern European countries, Russians, and others such as UK citizens = €550
    2. Middle Eastern countries = €350
    3. Asian/American countries = €850

The procedure usually takes 10 business days to obtain all the documents and submit the application. Then, the individual or family will schedule an appointment for immigration to obtain biometric data.

Permanent residence

There are 2 routes and it is valid for life, with no need for renewal.

It is not necessary to reside in Cyprus either before, during, or after the application.

The only requirement is that the applicant must visit Cyprus once every 2 years, unlike other European countries that insist on residing for at least 3 months a year.

It can also be issued to:

-Spouses.
-Dependent children under 18 years of age.
-Parents.

There are 2 options:

Fast-track (around 2-3 months).

-The main requirement is the purchase of a property in Cyprus with a total market value of at least €300,000 + 5% VAT.
The applicant must submit the application form accompanied by a sales contract and proof of payment of at least €200,000 + VAT.

The sales contract must have been deposited at the Cyprus Department of Lands and Surveys.

- It is necessary to demonstrate that there are annual incomes from abroad.

- A deposit of €30,000 must be placed in a Cypriot bank account and not withdrawn for at least three consecutive years.

Standard route (12-18 months).

- The main requirement is the purchase of a property in Cyprus without a specific value. The applicant must submit the application form accompanied by a sales contract and proof of payment.

- The sales contract must have been deposited at the Cyprus Department of Lands and Surveys.

- It is necessary to show that there are annual incomes from abroad.

- An account must be opened at a Cypriot banking institution.

Additional Requirements for Applying for Permanent Residence:

- Submit a clean criminal record certificate for all family members who are co-applicants.

- The applicant must not accept employment or engage in any profession or occupation in Cyprus and must submit a special form (declaration) confirming they have no intention to work or be engaged in any form of business in Cyprus.

- Submit a copy of a valid passport.

- Present evidence of stable income from abroad, property ownership abroad, and a statement from a Cypriot bank account.

- Submit a copy of a valid temporary residence permit (if the applicant resides in Cyprus).

- Submit a curriculum vitae (including academic qualifications) and all qualifications with diplomas.

- Proof of health insurance in Cyprus.

- Be present at the immigration authorities to obtain biometric data within a period of one year from the day approval was obtained.

- Minimum annual income of €30,000 from salaries from abroad, pensions, stock participation, rentals ...
The minimum annual income increases by €5,000 for each dependent person.

- All documents must be translated into English or Greek and notarized.

Frequently Asked Questions:

- Are permanent residence holders required to pay Cypriot taxes on their international income?
No, unless they spend more than 183 days in Cyprus per year. There are significant tax advantages for foreigners who become tax residents of Cyprus.

-What is the procedure for a Permanent Residence holder to apply for Citizenship based on years of residence?
The investor must have completed 7 years of legal residence in Cyprus before the date of the application and have resided legally and continuously in Cyprus for the 12 months prior to the application date.

-Who are considered economically dependent adult children?
Unmarried children aged between 18 and 25, who can prove they have been university students for at least 6 months after the date of the application.

-What if Permanent Residence "for life" is needed for dependents?
Children who are economically dependent can submit a separate application to obtain "lifetime" Permanent Residence.
In this case, parents must prove an additional income of at least €5,000 for each dependent child.

Permanent Residence "for life" will remain valid even after the child turns 25 years old and even if they are no longer single and/or a student and/or economically dependent. However, "lifetime" Permanent Residence will not be inherited by future generations.

10

COMPANY VAT REGISTRATION + COMPANY TAX REGISTRATION + COMPANY MANAGEMENT REGISTRATION.

-Company VAT Registration

This is the process by which a company registers with the relevant tax authority to obtain a VAT (Value Added Tax) identification number.

This number is necessary for the company to be able to charge VAT on the sales of goods and services and to deduct the VAT paid on its purchases.

It is essential for compliance with tax laws.

It allows the company to operate legally by collecting VAT and fulfilling reporting and payment obligations to tax authorities.

To proceed with the company's VAT registration, a sample invoice must be completed in which the new Cyprus company provides services to a company in the European Union for an amount of €100.

The invoice does not need to be real.

We will send you the invoice model for you to complete with your details and send back to us.

-Company tax registration

This process involves registering the company with the tax authority to comply with all corporate tax obligations, beyond VAT.

This includes income taxes, payroll taxes, and any other relevant corporate taxes.

It ensures that the company is recognized by the tax authorities and is in a position to comply with its tax obligations, including the payment of corporate taxes and the filing of tax returns.

Once the Yellow Slips are processed, we can proceed with the TIC (Tax Identification Code) for the company.

We will notify you when the tax department sends you the tax and identification numbers of the company by email.

The email you receive must be forwarded to us within a maximum of 2 hours to prevent expiration and to continue with the processing of the COMPANY TIC.

Information needed for processing:

-Your company's email address.

-<u>Company management registration</u>

This involves the registration of the company in terms of internal management or the information of directors and managers with regulatory or commercial authorities.

This includes the submission of documents detailing the company's structure, its directors, and any significant changes in management.

It facilitates transparency and regulatory compliance, allowing stakeholders, including banks, investors, and regulatory authorities, to access vital information about the management and structure of the company.

11
PERSONAL TAX REGISTRATION (PERSONAL TIC).

In Cyprus, "Personal Tax Registration" refers to the process by which an individual registers with the country's tax authority to fulfill their personal tax obligations.

This registration is necessary for anyone who has taxable income in Cyprus, including both residents and certain non-residents who generate income within the country.

Once registered, the individual receives a Tax Identification Number (TIN) which must be used for all transactions and communications with the tax authority.

This number is essential for filing income tax returns, paying taxes, and fulfilling other personal tax obligations.

Who needs to register?

-**Tax residents in Cyprus:** Individuals who spend more than 183 days in the country during the fiscal year are considered tax residents. These individuals are subject to tax on their global income.

-**Non-residents with income in Cyprus:** Those who do not meet the residency criterion but generate income in Cyprus through various sources, such as employment, rentals, or business activities, also need to register to comply with the tax obligations associated with those incomes.

Registering for personal tax is crucial for several reasons:

-**Legal compliance:** Ensures that the individual complies with Cyprus tax laws, avoiding penalties and fines.

-**Tax declaration and payment:** Facilitates the timely filing of income tax returns and the payment of any due taxes.

-**Tax benefits and deductions:** Allows the taxpayer to claim any deductions, credits, or tax benefits to which they are entitled.

-**Financial transactions:** A tax identification number is often required for various financial and legal transactions within the country.

Once the Yellow Slips have been processed, we can proceed with the Personal TIC.

We will notify you when the tax department sends you the tax and personal identification numbers by email.

You will need to forward that email to us within a maximum of 2 hours before it expires so that we can continue with the processing of the PERSONAL TIC.

You will receive the individual's TIC number in the indicated email, so the consultancy does not have to send any additional documents to the client.

Information needed for processing:

-Personal email or a different one from the company's.
-Phone number from the country of origin or Cyprus.
-Passport photos.
-Identity document photos.
-Utility bill (water or electricity) from the country of origin before residing in Cyprus.
-Current selfie photo: Required as proof for the application.
-Social security number photo (SIP in the case of Spain).

12

INTRACOMMUNITY OR CROSS-BORDER VAT (INCLUDES VIES)

Intracommunity or cross-border VAT refers to the Value Added Tax (VAT) regime applicable to transactions of goods and services between member countries of the European Union (EU).

This system is designed to facilitate trade within the European single market, allowing for efficient and simplified tax treatment of cross-border commercial operations between companies registered in different Member States.

The VIES (VAT Information Exchange System) plays a central role in this process.

What is VIES?

The VAT Information Exchange System (VIES) is a database maintained by the European Commission that allows tax authorities in EU Member States to verify the validity of VAT numbers of companies engaged in intracommunity transactions.

Its main objective is to prevent tax fraud in trade between EU countries and to facilitate VAT-free operations for registered businesses.

Once the "Company VAT Registration" is processed, we can proceed with the VIES registration.

There are four scenarios to consider for the application of intracommunity VAT:

-If your customer (business or individual) has a European VAT number, then the VAT rate is 0%.

-If your customer (business or individual) is outside the European Union, the VAT rate is 0%.

-If your customer (business or individual) is in the European Union and does not have a VAT number, a 19% rate is applied.

-If your customer is a company in Cyprus, a 19% rate is applied.

13

SALARY

Here are the two most interesting options regarding choosing the monthly salary you should set for yourself:

a) You can receive a monthly salary as consultancy fees.

You can receive an amount of €15,600 annually (€1,300 monthly) as salary, but it must be recorded as consultancy fees. When transferring these amounts, the description for the bank must indicate that they are "consultancy fees," not salary.

Example transfer description: "Pedro López Consultancy Fees March 2024".

The corresponding tax for the €15,600 annually is 2.65%, reflected at the end of the year in the payment of dividends from the company to the partner-shareholder.

There is no need to pay any self-employment fee nor is there any withholding from the salary or income tax.

It is important to have comprehensive health insurance which can range from €300-600 per year, as this option does not cover public health expenses or pension.

b) You can receive a conventional monthly salary.

To have a Social Security number, you must be registered with the Cyprus Social Security Department as an employee of your company.

You will be required to pay contributions on the salary each month.

Example: €1000 (salary) x 26.85% (rate) = €268.50 contribution each month.

In the monthly transfer, you should describe it as salary.

To qualify for the pension plan, you need to have social security for 15 years in Cyprus and accumulate 33 1/3 units.

14
IP BOX

Companies can benefit from more favorable tax treatment on income derived from intellectual property, such as patents, copyrights, trademarks, industrial designs, ...

In practice, the IP Box process involves the creation and approval of a project that we develop for a useful and original software tailored to your business, which must be used for your conventional economic activity.

If you have software, you will complete a questionnaire about it.

If you do not have software, we will help you create a project and guide you through everything necessary to then present it to the Cypriot Public Administration, ensuring it meets all the required conditions.

The IP Box process takes approximately 2 months (completion of the Resolution and response from the tax department), but an additional 2-3 weeks must be added for the second company registration that is necessary to process the IP Box.

Benefits: There is a reduction in the corporate tax rate from the standard 12.5% to 2.50%, for all economic activities conducted through the software.

To avail of the tax benefits, a second company must be created in Cyprus to hold the IP Box. The first company, which invoices the income and expenses, transfers the profits to this new company for management under the concept of intellectual property.

The VAT number will be shared by both the first company created in Cyprus and the second company created in Cyprus, which holds the IP Box.

A new bank account must be opened for the second company that will hold the IP Box.

Necessary information for the creation of the 2nd company that holds the IP Box:

-3 possible names for the company listed in order of preference.

If you want to expedite the process (approximately 7-14 days), you can indicate this, and we will show you different names already purchased by the advisory service for you to choose from and transfer to you.

-Paragraph describing the business in English.

-Photos of ID and passport.

-Name of the company director (there can be 2 partners as directors).

-Name of the company secretary (there can be only 1 secretary).

-If there are several partners-shareholders, the percentage of shares each one holds in the new company must be determined.

Finally, to process the Tax Identification Code (TIC) for this new company, we need:

-New email address.

15
ACCOUNTING

Depending on the volume of invoices, receipts, and the complexity of your accounting, the approximate price ranges from €1500-€3000 annually, excluding VAT, which is 19%.

This price includes the accounting services for both the company and the individual.

Additionally, there is an annual audit fee of €1000, as audits are mandatory in Cyprus, excluding VAT.

Accounting is submitted quarterly.

Procedure to follow:

Within the first 5-10 days after the end of the current accounting quarter, an email should be sent to the assigned person in the accounting department with all receipts, invoices, etc., for income and expenses, along with a detailed bank statement of all transactions for the quarter. Legally, the advisory service has 1 month and 10 days after the end of the quarter to submit your accounting.

Deductible expenses:

Phone, internet, IT, printing, stationery, meals for one or more persons (restaurant or bar meals and dinners), gasoline, supermarket food expenses (as long as they are outside Cyprus), taxi, hotel, flights, complete trips...

16
INVESTMENT: CRYPTOCURRENCIES, ETFs, TRADING, STOCK MARKET...

Cyprus has been considered an attractive destination for investors and companies, thanks to its favorable tax regime, membership in the European Union, and strategic position between Europe, Asia, and Africa. Below, we explain the situation regarding cryptocurrencies, ETFs, trading, and the stock market.

Cryptocurrencies:

The tax treatment of cryptocurrencies in Cyprus has been in the process of clarification, as in many other countries.

The holding and investment in cryptocurrencies were not explicitly regulated, but the income generated from related trading activities was considered taxable like any other business or investment gain.

This implies that both capital gains and income from cryptocurrency trading activities are subject to corporate tax and profit distribution:

-Corporate tax: Companies engaged in cryptocurrency trading are subject to the standard corporate tax in Cyprus, which is 12.5%, but it can be optimized with the IP BOX to just 2.50%, one of the lowest in the European Union.

-Dividend distribution: For individuals, profit distribution is taxed at 2.65%.

ETFs, Trading, and Stock Market:

Taxation on investments in ETFs, stocks, and other financial instruments in Cyprus is structured around corporate tax for companies, and capital gains tax for individuals.

-Corporate tax: Capital gains from the sale of securities, stocks, bonds, and other securities listed on any stock exchange are exempt from capital gains tax.
However, there are exceptions and specific conditions, so it is important to consult with a tax advisor.

-Dividends: Cyprus has a favorable regime for the taxation of dividends. Dividends received by Cypriot companies from their investments are exempt from corporate tax and subject to a 2.65% contribution.

-Interest: Interest earned from investments (other than interest generated in the normal course of business) is subject to a 2.65% profit distribution tax.

17
BANK ACCOUNTS

To choose a bank for your company and also for personal use, we suggest the following options:

a) Neobanks:

This is the best option as they have very low fees and you can operate without issues in Cyprus.

Here are the most interesting options for a **business account:**

-Revolut: This is the best option due to the services it offers. Additionally, they ensure up to €100,000 of your capital in case of bankruptcy.
-Worldfirst
-Airwallex
-Icard
-Vivawallet

Here are the most interesting options for a **personal account:**

-Revolut: This is the best option due to the services it offers. Additionally, they ensure up to €100,000 of your capital in case of bankruptcy.
-Blackcatcard
-Wirex
-Tap
-Broker: Freedom Finance
-Broker: Etoro

b) Traditional banks in Cyprus:

To open an account, you need to process quite a bit of documentation with these banks, and the banking fees are not very attractive for the service they provide.

Here are the most interesting options for **both corporate and personal accounts:**

-Eurobank
-Bank of Cyprus

If you would like to receive more information or open an account with any of these banks, let us know and we will send you all the required documentation.

If you decide to go with one of these traditional banks, a specialized person from the consultancy will assist you.

18

REAL ESTATE: RENTING AND BUYING PROPERTY

Online portals where you can find housing for rent or purchase in Cyprus:

1. Holprop
2. Properstar
3. Bazaraki.com Portal
4. Facebook Marketplace

Real estate agencies.

We have a trusted real estate agency that provides quality service throughout Cyprus.

Additionally, they can send a video of the property of interest and then a video call of the same for your security if you wish to secure the property from your country of origin and have the rental property available immediately upon your arrival in Cyprus.

If you are interested in exploring the properties they have available, without any commitment, let us know and we will put you in contact with them.

Buying property.

The following information should be considered:

The bank issuing the payment must be a physical bank, preferably part of the SWIFT network, as payments for property purchases cannot be made from a Neobank.

This is due to the requirements of banks in Cyprus, as they conduct due diligence procedures to verify the source of the funds.

For the purchase and sale of the property, the process usually takes about 3-4 months.

Other possibilities:

If you are interested in renting a room in an apartment to reside just 2 months a year and benefit from the entire tax system in Cyprus, we also offer this service, just ask us about it.

Considerations to keep in mind:

The physical address of the first property rented or purchased must be in the name of the individual as a resident in Cyprus for tax residency reasons.

You can also include the company name in the rental agreement, but it is essential that the name and identification number of the individual appear.

You can deduct as an expense 20% of the rental amount for each partner of the company, even if the contract is in the name of an individual.

The company can pay the total amount of the bills and classify them as expenses.

However, if the invoices are in the name of the company, you can claim the entire amount of VAT, but if they are in your personal name, you can only claim 1/3 of the VAT amount.

19
SETTING UP ELECTRICITY SUPPLY

In Cyprus, all rental properties require the tenant to set up the electricity when they move in.

Electricity is activated on the same day you access the property.

The landlord usually accompanies the tenant to complete the procedure.

Once the electricity service is contracted, supply is available the same day.

To set up the electricity supply, you must pay a deposit of €200 to the Cypriot public administration at the same location where the service is contracted, which is refunded when you leave the dwelling.

Electricity bills are paid every 2 months.

For tax residency reasons, the electricity supply must be registered in the name of the individual.

Regarding electricity expenses, since it will be in your name as an individual, you can deduct 1/3 of the total amount as a business expense.

The company can pay the total amount of the bills and classify them as expenses.

However, if the invoices are in the name of the company, it can claim the entire amount of VAT; if they are in your personal name, it can only claim 1/3 of the VAT amount.

20
SETTING UP WATER SUPPLY

In Cyprus, all rental properties require the tenant to set up the water service when they move in.

Water service is activated on the same day you access the property.

The landlord usually accompanies the tenant to complete the procedure.

Once the water service is contracted, supply is available the same day.

To set up the water supply, you must pay a deposit of €200 to the Cypriot public administration at the same location where the service is contracted, which is refunded when you leave the dwelling.

Water bills are paid every 3 months.

For residency reasons, the water supply must be registered in the name of the individual.

Regarding water expenses, since it will be in your name as an individual, you can deduct 1/3 of the total amount as a business expense.

The company can pay the total amount of the bills and classify them as expenses.

However, if the invoices are in the name of the company, it can claim the entire amount of VAT; if they are in your personal name, it can only claim 1/3 of the VAT amount.

21

INSURANCE: HEALTH AND VEHICLE

We have contact with a trusted insurance agency specialized in foreigners, which offers insurance services throughout Cyprus.

If you are interested in getting a quote, let us know and we will put you in touch with them.

Frequent questions about health insurance:

-Health insurance can be paid in 12 installments per year.

-With regular health insurance, after obtaining a card or policy, you can use it within their network of medical center facilities. However, if you have an emergency, you should go directly to the nearest hospital. Any other procedure must be pre-authorized.

-It is not possible to include 2 or more people on the same health insurance policy as they are individual policies.

-Regarding the "€50 Mandatory Deductible," it means that the €50 is a one-time payment for the first medical service, after which the insurance will cover up to the contracted limit.

-If we choose the option "Area 3 - Cyprus, Europe, Israel," the insurance will cover procedures in any of the three regions, but only up to the cost of the procedure in Cyprus.

-We have to pay the medical expenses ourselves, and then the insurance reimburses us in our bank account up to the insurance limit if we choose a doctor outside of the network of facilities included in the insurance, but within the network, you only have to show your card or policy.

To request a health insurance quote, the following information needs to be provided:

- Insured's Name.
- Date of Birth.
- Nationality.
- Identification Number (ID).
- Passport Number.
- Complete Address in Cyprus.
- Occupation.

For a car insurance quote, the following information needs to be provided:

- Vehicle.
- License Plate.
- Value of the Vehicle.
- Coverages to be included.
- Start Date of the Insurance.

- Vehicle Owner's Name.
- Identification Number (ID).
- Complete Address in Cyprus.

- Main Driver's Name.
- Date of Birth.
- Nationality.
- Identification Number.
- Passport Number.
- Driver's License Issue Date.
- Complete Address in Cyprus.

- Occasional Driver's Name.
- Date of Birth.
- Nationality.
- Identification Number.
- Passport Number.
- Driver's License Issue Date.
- Complete Address in Cyprus.

- For insurance policy holder (Policyholder).
- Name.
- Identification Number.
- Date of Birth.
- Nationality.
- Driver's License Issue Date.

- Insurance company in the country of origin that is currently active.
- Policy Number.
- Vehicle Model.
- License Plate.

Important notice: It is very important to provide a no-claims bonus document from the current insurance holder's company so that a discount can be applied and the insurance can be processed smoothly. Without this document, most insurance companies in Cyprus refuse to issue the policy. You can request this document from your insurance company in your country of origin, and they will send it to you at no cost.

To contract car insurance, the company requests:

- Passport copy of all drivers.
- ID copy of all drivers.
- Driver's license copy of all drivers.
- Copy of the vehicle registration document (Copy of logbook).
- Copy of no-claims bonus of the policyholder and/or main driver.

22

VEHICLE RENTAL AND PURCHASE

Vehicle rental by minutes and hours:

The quickest option, if you will use the car occasionally, is to rent vehicles with the company Ride Now through their APP or their website: https://ridenow.tech/

RideNow is the first carsharing service in Cyprus, offering an efficient and flexible option for residents and tourists to rent cars for short periods, from a few minutes to several days.

You can pick up and return the vehicles at various locations, including cities like Larnaca, Limassol, Paphos, Nicosia, and at both Larnaca and Paphos airports.

Using the RideNow app, you can unlock cars and manage your rentals.

The service includes the costs of fuel, taxes, and basic insurance, though you have the option to upgrade to extended insurance to reduce liability.

An internet connection is essential to unlock and lock the cars through the app, which is especially important since some areas in Cyprus may have poor internet coverage.

The pricing is based on time and distance with options to rent by the minute, hour, or day.

There are various packages available that can be tailored to your needs, and prices are higher for drivers under 25 years old due to insurance policies.

It takes 1-2 days to validate you, after which you can use the service.

Portals where we can contact car sellers:

-Facebook Marketplace.
-Bazaraki.com
-Dealerships and second-hand vehicle stores.

Interesting:

We have the contact of a trusted dealership that sells new cars from brands like Mercedes, Alfa Romeo, Fiat, Jeep, Peugeot, Citroën, and Opel. If you come referred by us, they can offer you a special discount.

They also have a small stock of second-hand cars and collaborate with a car leasing company.

If you are interested in reviewing, without any commitment, the vehicles they have available, let us know and we will put you in contact with them.

Tips:

-For Europeans, it is better to buy an automatic car since the gear shift is on the left, although it is a bit more expensive.

-If you are interested in buying a second-hand car, it is very important that you buy from a private individual or a completely trustworthy company, as a large percentage of second-hand cars sold in Cyprus have problems.

If you decide to buy a second-hand car on your own, before making the purchase, it is very important to request:

-Vehicle maintenance history.
-Test drive.
-Pre-purchase inspection by a professional workshop.

Before proceeding with the vehicle purchase, you must have:

-MOT (equivalent to the vehicle inspection in Spain, conducted every 2 years in Cyprus).
-ROAD TAX (Tax that is obtained at the road transport office).

To proceed with the purchase transaction, you must have:

- Transfer of Ownership: This is filled out at a specialized management office.
- Registration Certificate.
- Active Car Insurance (new owner).
- Passports.
- If you are purchasing the car in the name of a company, you need the company's seal for stamping.

The seal can be made at a locksmith company that manufactures keys for housing, and you must include the company's name and commercial registry number. It is advisable to also include the Tax Identification Number (TIN) and the full address where the company is fiscally located.

Important:

All these documents are presented at the citizen service offices where they will be stamped.

It is necessary that the previous owner of the vehicle you have just purchased accompanies you to also make some signatures.

Renewing the road tax:

- Must be done once a year.
- The approximate cost is €66 per year.

Link to renew the road tax:

https://rtd.mcw.gov.cy/WebPhase1/gui/Common/LoginFrameGreek.jsp?lang=en

23

COMPANIES: INTERNET AND PHONE

You can sign up for mobile phone and internet services in Cyprus online, by phone, or in person at one of the numerous offices of the companies providing these services.

Our advice is to visit an office in person because often the online rates are outdated, but when you go to a physical office, they can present great offers, in addition to providing ADSL or fiber optic services, depending on where you will be residing.

The three most important phone and internet companies to consider are:

-CYTA:

It is the largest company in Cyprus.

Web links:

https://www.cyta.com.cy/about/en
https://www.cyta.com.cy/internet-home-products/en
https://www.cyta.com.cy/mobile-plans/en

Landline: +357 22 880 132

-EPIC:

It is the second-largest company in Cyprus.

Web link: https://www.epic.com.cy/en/page/start/home

-PRIMETEL:

It is the 3rd largest company in Cyprus.

Website link: https://primetel.com.cy

If the procedure is carried out in the name of the company, the following documentation must be presented:

-Company documents such as the constitution, director and secretary document...

-Company seal: The seal can be made at a locksmith that manufactures house keys and you must include the name of the company and the commercial registration number.
It is also advisable to include the Tax Identification Number (TIN) and the full address where the company is fiscally located.

-Housing rental contract: If the internet is registered in the name of the company, which is most advisable for deducting the entire expense, the rental contract must also include the company in addition to your individual name.

If the procedure is carried out in the name of an individual, the following documentation must be presented:

-Passport.
-Personal identification document (ID).
-Housing rental contract.

24
COWORKING SPACES.

If you are a freelancer, entrepreneur, or digital nomad looking for a place to work and socialize with others, Cyprus is your ideal destination.

This Mediterranean island country offers a wide variety of coworking spaces that cater to different needs, budgets, and lifestyles.

Here are 10 coworking places in Cyprus:

-Hub Nicosia: This space is located in the capital of Cyprus, Nicosia. It offers a creative, collaborative, and community-oriented environment. It features meeting rooms, lounge areas, a kitchen, a library, and regular events. Prices range from €10 per day to €120 per month.

-The Cookhouse: Located in Limassol, it combines a professional kitchen with a workspace. You can rent a cooking station by the hour or by the day, and enjoy dishes prepared by other members or yourself.
There is also a conference room, a terrace, and a cafe. Prices range from €15 per day to €200 per month.

-Impact Hub Limassol: Situated in Limassol, it is part of a global network of Impact Hubs. It offers flexible workspaces, with individual or shared desks, meeting rooms, events, and workshops. Prices start from €12 per day to €150 per month.

- **Regus:** This company has several locations in Cyprus such as Nicosia, Limassol, and Larnaca. It offers private offices, dedicated desks, meeting rooms, reception services, and access to a global network of workspaces. Prices vary depending on the location and type of service.

- **Cocoon:** This space is located in the historic center of Nicosia and has a modern and minimalist design. It features individual and shared desks, meeting rooms, common areas, a kitchen, and cultural events. Prices range from €15 per day to €180 per month.

- **Home for Cooperation:** Located in a special area, it is situated in the neutral zone that separates the Greek and Turkish parts of Nicosia. It is a multicultural and multilingual space. It offers individual and shared desks, meeting rooms, a library, a café, and social events. Prices range from €5 per day to €80 per month.

- **Gravity Ventures:** This space in Nicosia specializes in supporting startups and entrepreneurs with innovative ideas. It offers an acceleration program that includes mentorships, funding, access to a network of experts, and workspaces. There are also networking events, workshops, and talks. Prices start from €20 per day to €250 per month.

- **The Home Project:** Located in Larnaca, it has a cozy and homely atmosphere. It offers individual and shared desks, meeting rooms, common areas, a kitchen, and educational events. Prices range from €10 per day to €120 per month.

-The Business Bar: Located in Paphos, it features elegant and sophisticated decor.
It offers individual and shared desks, meeting rooms, common areas, a bar, and professional events.
Prices range from €15 per day to €200 per month.

-Co-working Latchi: Situated in Latchi, it offers a spectacular view of the Mediterranean Sea.
It features individual and shared desks, meeting rooms, common areas, a kitchen, and sports activities.
Prices range from €10 per day to €100 per month.

25
HOME DELIVERY.

These are the companies in Cyprus that can deliver food to your home, by downloading their app on your mobile phone:

-Wolt: A Finnish food delivery company that began operations in Cyprus in 2020. The company offers a wide range of services through its app, including restaurant food delivery and grocery shopping. In Cyprus, Wolt operates in various cities like Nicosia, Limassol, Larnaca, Paphos, partnering with over 2,000 restaurants and local businesses to provide a diverse variety of food products and retail items. Wolt also offers a subscription service called Wolt+, which provides benefits such as zero delivery fees on eligible orders from restaurants and stores, along with exclusive offers and discounts. This subscription is designed to pay for itself after just a few orders each month due to savings on delivery fees. The company has made significant contributions to the Cypriot economy by supporting local businesses and creating jobs, which has helped to cement its popularity among consumers in Cyprus.

–Foody Cyprus: A popular delivery app in Cyprus that allows users to order food, groceries, and other items for home delivery or pickup. The platform supports a wide variety of cuisines, working in collaboration with both local and national chains, providing users with an extensive selection of culinary options. A standout feature of Foody is its focus on ease of use and convenience. The app's interface is designed to make the process of placing orders and tracking delivery status as simple and efficient as possible.
This aligns with the current trend of food delivery apps, which aim to enhance the user experience by minimizing complications and maximizing efficiency. In addition to offering food delivery services, Foody in Cyprus also extends to the delivery of groceries and other essential products, thus providing a comprehensive solution for the daily needs of consumers.

26
NATIONALITY.

Acquiring Cypriot nationality can be achieved through several methods, including naturalization, descent, marriage, and investment.

Here are the general requirements and some specifics for the most common methods of acquiring nationality in Cyprus:

By naturalization:

Naturalization is one of the most common methods for obtaining citizenship in many countries, including Cyprus.

The requirements include:

-Legal residence: The individual must have legally resided in Cyprus for a specific period before applying. In Cyprus, this period is generally 7 years for most applicants, but it is reduced to 5 years for spouses of Cypriot citizens. However, for individuals of Cypriot descent, the required period may be shorter.

-Good conduct: Demonstrate good conduct and have no serious criminal record in Cyprus or any other country.

-Knowledge of the greek language: Demonstrate adequate knowledge of Greek, which is the official language of the Republic of Cyprus.

-Means of subsistence: Demonstrate the ability to support oneself and one's family, if applicable.

-Documentation:

Applying for nationality requires the compilation and preparation of some official documents:

- Applicant's birth certificate.
- Marriage/divorce certificates (if applicable).
- Proof of legal residence in Cyprus (e.g., residence permits).
- Certificate of clean criminal record, both from Cyprus and the applicant's country of origin.
- Proof of sufficient knowledge of the Greek language (for naturalization applications).
- Evidence of sufficient financial means to live in Cyprus without being a burden on the state.
- Any other document that may support the application, such as evidence of integration into Cypriot society.

-Submission of the application:

Once all necessary documents are collected, the application and supporting documents must be submitted to the Ministry of Interior of Cyprus or the designated local authority. An application fee is required.

-Assessment process:

After submission, the application enters an assessment process, where authorities review the documentation, assess compliance with the requirements, and may conduct interviews or further investigations if deemed necessary.

- **Decision and oath of allegiance:**

If the application is approved, the applicant will be notified of the decision and asked to take an oath of allegiance to the Republic of Cyprus. After this step, the naturalization certificate will be granted, thus completing the process of acquiring Cypriot nationality.

Additional considerations.

- **Legal consultation:** Given the complexity of the process and the possibility of changes in legislation, it is advisable to consult with a lawyer specializing in immigration or nationality law who can provide advice and personalized assistance. We can help you with the process.

- **Processing time:** The processing time for nationality applications can vary significantly, depending on the workload of the authorities, the complexity of the case, and the completeness of the documentation submitted.

By descent:

Individuals with Cypriot ancestry can apply for citizenship based on their descent.

This includes those born abroad to parents (or in some cases, grandparents) who are Cypriot citizens.

The required documents generally include birth and marriage certificates, and if necessary, proof of Cypriot citizenship of the parents or grandparents.

By marriage:

Spouses of Cypriot citizens can also apply for nationality after a specific period of marriage and residence in the country.

The requirements include:

-Duration of marriage: Generally, the marriage must have lasted at least 3 years, and the couple must have lived in Cyprus for at least 2 years prior to the application.

-Documentation: Submit marriage certificates, residence proofs, and other documents that verify the authenticity of the marriage and cohabitation.

By investment:

Cyprus had programs that allowed the acquisition of citizenship through significant investments in the country. However, it is important to note that the Citizenship by Investment (CBI) program was abolished in November 2020 following controversies and criticisms, due to the large influx of Russians through this system.

27
SECURITY.

Discover the peace of mind of doing business in Cyprus, a paradise not only for its climate and natural beauty but also for its impressive security.

In Cyprus, security is such a part of daily life that in many villages and small towns, it is common for residents to leave their doors open during the day and their cars unlocked with the keys in overnight.

Imagine the peace of leaving your bicycle on the beach promenade without a lock, enjoying a sunny day of swimming, and returning to find it just where you left it.

Thus, Cyprus maintains its reputation as one of the safest countries in the European Union, with crime rates that are enviably low compared to other member states, making Cyprus an attractive destination to live, work, and study.

According to the 2023 Numbeo safety report, Cyprus consistently ranked well in terms of low crime perception and high safety perception when walking alone during the day and night, being the safest country in the European Union.

The 7 countries with the highest crime rate within the European Union are:

1. France
2. Belgium
3. Sweden
4. Greece
5. United Kingdom
6. Italy
7. Ireland

Additionally, Cyprus has one of the lowest rates of violent and serious crimes.

According to Eurostat in 2023, the statistical agency of the European Union, the 7 countries with the highest rates of violent crimes are:

1. Sweden
2. Denmark
3. Finland
4. France
5. Belgium
6. Italy
7. Germany

28

EDUCATION.

Currently, parents can choose between the local educational system or private and international schools, with the latter being the better option.

Here are the main aspects:

PUBLIC EDUCATIONAL SYSTEM.

-Access to education: Cyprus offers free public education access to all children residing in the country, including those from foreign parents, from preschool to secondary education. Education is compulsory for all children between the ages of 5 and 15 years. This reflects the country's commitment to educational rights under various international conventions.

-Language of instruction: Greek is the primary language of instruction in public schools in Cyprus. This can pose a challenge for children of foreign parents who do not speak this language, however, schools often offer additional language classes such as English to help students integrate.

PRIVATE AND INTERNATIONAL SCHOOLS.

For families who prefer or need another option, there are numerous private and international schools in Cyprus that teach most classes in English and other languages, following international programs such as the International Baccalaureate (IB) or British education (GCSE and A-Levels).

These schools typically attract a diverse student population, including many children from foreign families.

Types of private schools:

In Cyprus, private and international schools always conduct all classes in English, except for one subject which is Greek, and they mainly offer two different types of education:

-International baccalaureate (IB): An internationally recognized program that promotes critical thinking and a global mindset.

-British education: Includes the GCSE (General Certificate of Secondary Education) and A-Levels, highly valued for their academic rigor and broad university recognition.

Examples of private schools:

Limassol:

-Pascal english school: Offers British education and the International Baccalaureate, preparing students for higher education in Cyprus and abroad.
-Limassol international school: Known for its focus on the holistic development of the student, it offers an education that combines elements of British teaching with international educational approaches.

Nicosia:

-The G.C. school of careers: Founded in 1973, it offers a comprehensive educational program based on British education from primary education to A-Levels.
-American academy nicosia: A private school that provides English education from preschool through A-Levels, with an emphasis on specialized student development.

Larnaca:

- **American academy Larnaca:** Founded in 1908, it is one of the oldest educational institutions offering English-language education with an emphasis on Christian values.
- **Med high private english school:** Provides education from preschool to A-Levels, with a program that prepares students for universities in Cyprus and worldwide.

Paphos:

- **International school of Paphos:** Offers education from early childhood to A-Levels, following British teaching and promoting academic excellence and personal development.

Costs:

Costs vary widely depending on the school, educational level, and additional services offered. Generally, tuition can range from a few thousand to over ten thousand euros per year.
It is essential to contact the schools directly for accurate information about prices and included services.
It should be noted that, in addition to tuition, there may be additional charges, such as registration, books, uniforms, and extracurricular activities.

Additional considerations:

- **Admission and requirements:** Admission policies vary between schools. Some may require entrance exams, interviews, or assessments of the student's previous academic performance.

- **Language:** Although the primary medium of instruction is English, schools often offer additional language classes, including Greek, to facilitate integration into the local environment.

- **Accreditations:** Seeking schools that are accredited by relevant international organizations, such as the Council of International Schools (CIS) or the International Baccalaureate Organization (IBO), can ensure high educational standards.

Examples of universities in Cyprus:

- **University of Cyprus:** Located in Nicosia, it is the country's premier higher education institution, offering a wide range of programs in both Greek and English. It is noted for its research and teaching in science, humanities, engineering, and social sciences.
- **Cyprus University of Technology:** Situated in Limassol, it specializes in technical and technological fields but also offers programs in communication sciences, arts, and economics. Its programs are designed to meet the demands of the modern job market.
- **European University Cyprus:** Offering educational programs including medicine, health sciences, engineering, social sciences, and humanities, this university in Nicosia is distinguished by its focus on innovation and academic excellence.
- **Open University of Cyprus:** Offers distance learning programs in various fields, making it ideal for students seeking flexibility in their education.
- **University of Nicosia:** Known for being a pioneer in offering medical programs and also for being the first university in the world to offer a Master's in Digital Currency.
The University of Nicosia attracts a large number of international students each year.

LEGAL AND PRACTICAL CONSIDERATIONS.

Legal and practical considerations for enrolling a child in the educational system in Cyprus, whether public or private/international, involve several steps and requirements that families must consider.

These considerations ensure that the enrollment process goes smoothly and that students can start their education in a new environment effectively.

Registration and Documentation:

-Birth certificates: An official birth certificate translated (if not in Greek or English) is required to enroll a child in any school. This document serves as proof of the child's age and, in some cases, the relationship with the parents or legal guardians.
-Proof of residence: Parents must provide proof of residence in Cyprus. This can be a rental agreement, a utility bill in their name, or any official document that proves their residential address on the island.
-Legal status: For children from foreign families, it is crucial to provide documentation that certifies the family's legal status in Cyprus. This may include residence permits, work visas, or similar documents.
-Academic history: For enrollment at higher levels, especially in the case of private and international schools, it may be necessary to present the child's academic record and certificates from previous education.

Enrollment Process.

-Visits and meetings: It is recommended to visit schools of interest to meet with the staff, see the facilities, and better understand the educational and social environment they offer.
-Applications and deadlines: Both public and private schools may have specific deadlines for enrollment. In the case of private and international institutions, the application process may include application forms, interviews, and, in some cases, entrance exams.

29

FREQUENTLY ASKED QUESTIONS

-Can we submit receipts for meal expenses, per diems, plane tickets, hotels, taxis, etc., from Spain where we are currently located, as well as from other countries, starting from the date of company creation in Cyprus?
Yes, you should also consider that meal expenses in Cyprus can be deducted up to 1% of the sales generated by your Cypriot company.

-Can food purchases made at a supermarket in a country other than Cyprus be submitted as an accounting expense for the company we have in Cyprus using the receipt or invoice?
Yes, you can submit them as company expenses.

-What other expenses can we submit within the company?
Phone, IT, printing, stationery.

-Is private health insurance deductible as a company expense in Cyprus? Yes.

-Do we need expense invoices, or are purchase receipts sufficient?
It is better if you have invoices, but purchase receipts or tickets are also valid.

-Do I need to be in Cyprus to start the procedure?
No, it is not necessary to be in Cyprus to start the company registration or tax residency procedure.

-Do I need to be in Cyprus to start invoicing?
No, you do not need to be in Cyprus to start invoicing.
You can operate your company from anywhere in the world.

-Do I need to have a bank account in Cyprus?
Not necessarily. We can provide you with a list of online banks that accept accounts for Cypriot companies.

-Can I choose my own company name?
Yes, it takes about 3 to 4 business days for the company name to be approved.

-How long does it take to establish the company?
It takes approximately one month to register the company and obtain a VAT number to issue your first invoice.

-How long does it take to establish tax residency?
The minimum is 60 days. The process can be carried out simultaneously with the company registration.

-I rent out a property I own in my home country. Do I pay taxes in Cyprus or in my home country?
This depends on the country where the property is located.
If the property is in Spain, you need to process the Modelo 210 and pay 19% tax on the rental income quarterly.

-When do I need to deregister from my home country?
As soon as we have your personal tax number in Cyprus, we will send it to you, and you can submit your deregistration request.

-Is it necessary to obtain the Tax Residency Certificate (TRC)?
We can request the TRC from the tax department only if someone asks for it, such as the Spanish authorities or a bank. It takes approximately 3-4 weeks to be issued. It can only be requested at the end of the year or at the beginning of the following year because until that date, we cannot prove to the tax authorities that you stayed in Cyprus for 60 or 183 days and therefore did not stay in any other country for more than 183 days. Sometimes clients need it in the first year because the Spanish or European authorities request it, but not always. The fees for the TRC are €500.

-Do I need a permanent address in Cyprus to obtain non-domicile status?
Yes, a permanent address is necessary, and you must have utility bills in your name. Studios or rooms are also acceptable; the important thing is to have a bill registered at the address.

It is the most economical option if you will be there for a short time.
If you are interested in this option, let us know and we will help you.

—Do the 60 days need to be consecutive?
No, the 60 days can be separated. For example, you can spend 20 days in March, 20 days in June, and 20 days in September.

—How do I close the company if I want to stop operating it?
We need to apply for a suspension which costs €600. The company is then published in the registrar's bulletin, and if there are no objections, the company is automatically dissolved after 6 months.

—What if I want to make changes to directors or shareholders?
Yes, you can make changes to the company's status. The changes take 5 business days to be processed.

—How do the Cypriot authorities know that I am in Cyprus?
The tax department will ask for bank statements to verify that you have made purchases with your card within the republic (e.g., supermarkets, shops, bars, restaurants).

—Can I have a personal account in another country?
Yes, of course, you can maintain all your personal bank accounts in different jurisdictions.

—What if I have too many personal expenses?
You can add some of your personal expenses under the company if they are related to the company's operations.

—Can I buy a car with the company's money?
Yes, it is possible to buy the car and add it as a company asset, but it is a taxable benefit. However, you can add expenses related to the car's operations when it is used for the company, such as fuel and servicing.

—When do I need to pay taxes?
A financial year in Cyprus starts on 01/01 and ends on 31/12. The standard tax rate is 12.5%, but it can be reduced to 2.50% with the IP Box regime if you use software in your company.

-How does the healthcare system work?

You have two options regarding the healthcare system:

The first option is to purchase private health insurance in Cyprus, which can range from €200 to €800 per year, depending on the coverage and the age of the insured.

The second option (preferable for families) is to pay yourself a salary and contribute to social security, which provides European benefits for the whole family, including children. The social security contribution is 25.8% of the salary as it covers both the employee and the employer.

-Can I have an employee in the company?

We recommend hiring independent freelancers to invoice your company, which pays them as subcontractors. You can also create an agreement between the company and the subcontractors, including the same rights and obligations as an employee, and even add working hours, annual leave, etc. It is most beneficial if they are freelancers in their country or have their own company to invoice you for their services.

-Can I receive a salary from the company?

Yes, we recommend receiving a salary as the company director up to €15,600 per year, which is equivalent to €1,300 per month. This way, you do not need to register or file any declarations as an individual. You can always receive a higher salary, but you will need to file an annual declaration as a freelancer, which is not recommended as you will pay more taxes.

-How can I connect with other expats from my country in Cyprus?

In Cyprus, there are several WhatsApp groups for Spaniards, Germans, and other expats who meet every weekend for excursions, meals, dinners, sports, etc. We will invite you to join these groups so you can subscribe to them.

- What taxes are there on inheritance, wealth, and donations?
There are no taxes on inheritance, wealth, or donations.

- When can I pay dividends or distribute company profits?
You can do it once a year or four times a year (each quarter); however, at the end of the year is most recommended.

- Can we register a trade name so that the company has rights over this name when we advertise the company?
Yes, you can register a trade name at a cost of €300 (current cost for the Tax Department).

- What number should be used for the company's income and expense invoices in Cyprus?
The Tax Identification Number (TIN) is the number you should use on both your sales and expense invoices. The company registration number should not be used for this purpose, although you can include it on your sales invoices if you wish.

- After 17 years of non-domiciled status, what taxes are paid when dividends are distributed from the company?
A 17% special defense tax on dividends plus 2.65% GESY, totaling 19.65%.

- Do I need social insurance?
It is not necessary to have social insurance to be a director of a company.

- Calculation of some days for tax residency in Cyprus:

1. The day of departure from Cyprus counts as a day of residency outside Cyprus.
2. The day of arrival in Cyprus counts as a day of residency in Cyprus.
3. Arriving and departing from Cyprus on the same day counts as a day of residency in Cyprus.
4. Departing and arriving in Cyprus on the same day counts as a day of residency outside Cyprus.

30

HISTORY OF CYPRUS.

The history of Cyprus is extensive and complex, marked by its strategic position in the Mediterranean, which has attracted many civilizations over the millennia.

ANCIENT HISTORY:

The prehistory and antiquity of Cyprus offer a fascinating glimpse into early civilizations and human development in the Mediterranean.

The island has played a crucial role in ancient history, mainly due to its rich source of copper, and its strategic location that facilitated trade and cultural interaction.

1. Prehistory:

-First settlements: The earliest evidence of human activity in Cyprus dates back to the 10th millennium BC, in the Neolithic period. These early inhabitants arrived from the mainland, introducing agriculture, animal husbandry, and the first forms of permanent settlement on the island.

-Neolithic: During this period (approximately 8200-3900 BC), Cyprus saw the development of significant settlements, such as Choirokoitia and Kalavasos-Tenta, which are UNESCO World Heritage Sites. These sites show evidence of advanced social organization, architecture of fortified circular dwellings, and agricultural and animal husbandry practices.

2. Bronze age:

-Copper trade: The Bronze Age (approximately 2500-1050 BC) transformed Cyprus into a major center of copper production and trade, a metal essential for the manufacture of tools and weapons throughout the region. Cypriot copper was highly coveted and was exported throughout the Mediterranean, boosting the economy and wealth of the island.
The name "Cyprus" derives from the Latin word "aes Cyprium," meaning "metal of Cyprus," referring to copper.
This term evolved into the Latin word "cuprum," from which the current chemical term for copper (Cu) is derived.
The wealth generated by the copper trade allowed Cyprus to establish trade and cultural relations with major Mediterranean civilizations, including the Egyptians, Assyrians, and Greeks. This fostered a cultural exchange that was reflected in the art, religion, and social practices of the island.

-Minoans and mycenaeans: Towards the end of the Bronze Age, Cyprus was influenced by the Minoans and later by the Mycenaean Greeks, who established settlements and promoted the use of Greek language, religion, and Hellenistic cultural practices, which have persisted to this day.
Additionally, throughout its ancient history, Cyprus was subject to control and conquest by various foreign powers, due to its strategic position and rich resources.
These included the Egyptians, Hittites, Assyrians, and Persians.

3. Greek hellenistic period:

-Conquest of Alexander the great: The Greek influence in Cyprus was solidified with the island's conquest by Alexander the Great in 333 BC. After his death, Cyprus became part of the empire of the Ptolemies of Egypt, maintaining close cultural and political relations with the Hellenistic world.

- **Ptolemaic governance:** Under the Ptolemies, one of Alexander the Great's generals, Cyprus played a strategic role in the Eastern Mediterranean, serving as a major naval and commercial hub. During this period, the cities of Cyprus experienced a cultural flourishing, with the construction of new temples, theaters, and other public buildings in the Greek style.

4. Roman period:

- **Annexation to the roman empire:** In 58 BC, Cyprus was annexed to the Roman Empire by Pompey. It became a senatorial province and, later, during the reign of Augustus, an imperial province. The Romanization of the island brought administrative changes and further urban development. During Roman rule, Cyprus enjoyed a long period of peace and prosperity. Infrastructure was improved, including roads, aqueducts, and ports, and magnificent public and private buildings were erected. Urban life flourished in cities like Paphos, Salamis, and Kourion.

- **Christianity:** Cyprus holds a special place in the history of early Christianity. According to the Acts of the Apostles, the apostles Paul, Barnabas (a native of Cyprus), and Mark visited the island on their first missionary journey, converting the Roman proconsul Sergius Paulus to Christianity. It is also said that Lazarus, resurrected by Jesus, preached until his death, where a church holds his supposed remains.
Thus, Cyprus became one of the first places in the Mediterranean to adopt Christianity as a religion, with a well-established ecclesiastical organization from an early stage. The Greco-Roman period in Cyprus was characterized by cultural coexistence and syncretism. Greek religious and cultural practices mixed with local traditions and Roman influences, creating a rich cultural melting pot.

The art and architecture of Cyprus during this period reflect the fusion of Greek and Roman influences. The mosaics of Paphos, for example, are evidence of the high level of Roman art on the island, while numerous archaeological sites reveal the continuity of Hellenistic traditions. The economy of Cyprus under Roman rule benefited from trade within the vast empire. The production and export of copper remained important, and the island was also known for its wines and other agricultural products.

MIDDLE AGES:

Byzantine Period: In Cyprus, this period spans approximately from the 4th to the 12th century. It represents an era of profound historical and cultural importance for the island. Throughout this time, Cyprus was firmly integrated into the Byzantine Empire, experiencing both periods of peace and prosperity as well as times of conflict and challenge.
The transition of Cyprus to Byzantine control occurred gradually after the division of the Roman Empire in 395 AD. Cyprus became part of the Eastern Roman Empire, later known as the Byzantine Empire, with Constantinople as its capital. During the Byzantine period, Orthodox Christianity was consolidated as the dominant religion in Cyprus.
The construction of Byzantine churches and monasteries, many of which are still preserved today, are a testament to the deep religious faith and artistic richness of the era. The religious architecture of this period is characterized by its elaborate mosaics, frescoes, and a distinctive architectural style that would influence the later development of religious architecture on the island.
From the 7th century, Cyprus faced numerous raids by the Arabs. In 649, the Arabs carried out a significant raid, marking the beginning of a period of recurrent conflicts.

In 688, Byzantine Emperor Justinian II and Umayyad Caliph Abd al-Malik signed a unique agreement under which Cyprus became a condominium, jointly administered and taxed by Byzantines and Arabs. This arrangement lasted until the Byzantines regained full control of the island in the 10th century. The definitive reconquest of Cyprus by the Byzantines led to a period of reconstruction and revitalization. Cities were fortified and new churches were built, reflecting the resurgence of Byzantine influence. During the period of Iconoclasm in the Byzantine Empire (726-787 and 814-842), Cyprus became a refuge for monks and Orthodox faithful who venerated icons, although the island itself was not immune to internal conflicts related to this controversy. Cyprus is home to some of the most impressive examples of Byzantine art, especially in the form of mosaics and frescoes in churches and monasteries.
These works are not only artistically valuable but also provide significant insights into the religious and social life of the time.

2. Frankish rule (kingdom of Cyprus): In 1191, during the Third Crusade, Richard the Lionheart of England captured Cyprus from Isaac Comnenus, who had declared himself an independent ruler of the island. Richard used Cyprus as a base for his crusade to the Holy Land; however, shortly after his conquest, he sold the island to the Knights Templar, and when they found it too challenging to maintain control, they sold it to Guy de Lusignan, a French noble.
Guy de Lusignan established the Kingdom of Cyprus, inaugurating a period of Frankish rule that would last until the 15th century. Under the Lusignan, Cyprus became a fief of the Holy Roman Empire and later of the Papacy, maintaining close ties with Western Europe. During the Frankish rule, the island was characterized by a feudal society and a strong influence of French and Latin culture and traditions.
Numerous Gothic churches and castles were built, and Catholic religious orders were established.

Despite European domination, the Greek Orthodox population maintained their faith and cultural practices, though often in a subordinate position.

3. Venetian rule:

In 1489, following the death of Queen Charlotte of Lusignan without heirs, Cyprus passed into the hands of the Republic of Venice through the marriage of Caterina Cornaro, heir to the throne of Cyprus, to a Venetian nobleman.
Venice sought to control Cyprus primarily for its strategic and economic importance in Mediterranean trade.
The Venetians focused on strengthening Cyprus's defenses to protect against the growing Ottoman threat.
Impressive fortifications were built in cities like Nicosia, Famagusta, and Kyrenia. The Venetian administration imposed a centralized government system, but it also generated discontent among the local population due to high taxes and economic exploitation.
Venetian rule over Cyprus came to an end in 1571 when the Ottoman fleet, under the command of Lala Mustafa Pasha, conquered the island after the siege of Famagusta. The heroic, yet ultimately unsuccessful resistance of the Venetian garrison in Famagusta marked the end of Venetian control in Cyprus.

MODERN AGE:

The Ottoman Empire captured Cyprus from the Republic of Venice in 1571, after a prolonged siege of the city of Famagusta. The conquest was part of the Ottoman expansion in the Mediterranean, aimed at controlling strategic trade routes and countering European Christian influence.
Under Ottoman rule, Cyprus was organized as an eyalet or province, with a governor appointed by the sultan.

The Ottoman administration implemented tax systems and laws based on the millet system, which allowed a certain degree of autonomy to non-Muslim religious communities.
Although the Ottomans were Muslim, they promoted a policy of relative religious tolerance.
The Greek Orthodox Church, for example, received legal recognition and was allowed to self-govern in internal matters, which strengthened its position in Cypriot society.
The economy of Cyprus under Ottoman rule experienced periods of decline due to a combination of factors such as increased taxes, neglect of infrastructure, and recurring plagues and famines.
These economic problems, coupled with an often inefficient administrative system, affected the lives of the local population.
The Ottoman conquest also brought significant demographic changes, including the arrival of Muslim Turkish settlers.
This altered the ethnic and religious composition of the island, laying the groundwork for the complex Greek-Turkish relations in Cyprus.
Throughout the Ottoman period, there were episodes of resistance and revolts by the Cypriot population, largely motivated by discontent with the Ottoman administration, high taxes, and repression.
The Ottoman era left a lasting cultural legacy in Cyprus, visible in architecture, cuisine, and traditions.
Mosques and Turkish baths in cities like Nicosia and Famagusta are examples of Ottoman architectural influence.

CONTEMPORARY HISTORY:

-Cyprus was ceded to the british empire by the ottoman empire:
This occurred in 1878, under the Cyprus Convention, allowing Britain to use the island as a military base to protect the route to India, its colonial jewel. Although initially Cyprus was leased to the United Kingdom, it was formally annexed in 1914 at the start of World War I when the Ottoman Empire joined the Central Powers.

During British rule, Cyprus was governed as a Crown colony. The British implemented a colonial administrative structure while maintaining certain Ottoman structures, such as the millet system for religious communities.

Under British rule, Cyprus experienced significant improvements in its infrastructure.

The British built roads, improved ports, introduced postal and telegraphic services, and established a legal system based on the British model.

The British administration also attempted to modernize the Cypriot economy, though with limited success.

Agriculture remained the main economic activity, but efforts were made to diversify the economy, including promoting tourism.

During the British colonial period, nationalist movements began to emerge in Cyprus. The majority Greek Cypriot community sought "Enosis," or union with Greece, inspired by the ideal of the Megali Idea, the dream of reviving the Byzantine Empire under Greek leadership. On the other hand, the Turkish Cypriot minority, influenced by Turkish nationalism and in response to the Enosis movement, began to advocate for "Taksim," or the division of the island between Greece and Turkey.

The British response to these movements was generally repressive, with periods of martial law, censorship, and exile of nationalist leaders. Tensions between the Greek and Turkish Cypriot communities intensified, often with British colonialism acting as an unintentional mediator between the two.

-Independence:

Independence was the result of a negotiated process involving Britain, Greece, and Turkey. The talks were conducted in a context of escalating violence on the island, especially the guerrilla campaign carried out by EOKA (National Organization of Cypriot Fighters), which fought for the union (Enosis) of Cyprus with Greece.

The independence of Cyprus was formalized through the Zurich and London Agreements in 1959, which established a framework for the creation of the Republic of Cyprus. These agreements aimed to ensure a balance between the Greek Cypriot and Turkish Cypriot communities, granting both certain political rights and security guarantees.
The Republic of Cyprus was established as a bicommunal republic, where power would be shared between the two main communities on the island. The president would be Greek Cypriot and the vice president Turkish Cypriot, with a veto power in certain areas of governance to protect the interests of both communities. The agreements also designated Greece, Turkey, and the United Kingdom as guarantor powers of the independence, territorial integrity, and security of Cyprus. This gave them the right to intervene on the island under certain circumstances, a point that would have significant implications in the future.
Despite hopes for peace and stability, tensions between the Greek and Turkish Cypriot communities soon emerged. Disputes over the interpretation and application of the constitution led to intercommunal clashes. The situation worsened, reaching a critical point in 1963-64 when armed clashes led to the intervention of the United Nations.
In response to the violence, the United Nations established the United Nations Peacekeeping Force in Cyprus (UNFICYP) in 1964, aimed at preventing further clashes. The presence of UNFICYP continues to this day. Cyprus's independence did not resolve the fundamental tensions between its constituent communities. Subsequent events, especially the 1974 coup d'état supported by Greece and the subsequent Turkish invasion, led to a de facto division of the island, a situation that remains to this day.

Since 1960, there have been numerous attempts to resolve the Cypriot conflict, including reunification plans under the auspices of the UN. However, differences over security, governance, and property issues have hindered progress towards a lasting solution.

Since the independence of Cyprus in 1960, tensions between the Greek Cypriot and Turkish Cypriot communities have been a constant, often exacerbated by the policies of their respective motherlands, Greece and Turkey.

On July 15, 1974, a coup d'état in Cyprus, led by the military junta then in power in Greece, overthrew President Makarios III, aiming for Enosis, or the union of Cyprus with Greece.

This act was the immediate pretext for Turkish intervention. Turkey, justifying its action on its right to intervene as a guarantor power according to the Zurich and London Agreements of 1959-60, launched a military invasion on July 20, 1974, called "Operation Attila." The invasion occurred in two phases, the first starting on July 20 and the second on August 14, extending Turkish control to the north of the island.

The invasion led to a massive displacement of populations, with Greek Cypriots fleeing to the south and Turkish Cypriots to the north, exacerbating the island's ethnic division.

There were also numerous casualties and missing persons on both sides, and human rights violations were reported.

As a result of the invasion, Cyprus was de facto divided into two parts: the Republic of Cyprus, controlled by Greek Cypriots, covering approximately 59% of the southern part of the island, and the north, controlled by Turkish Cypriots and Turkish troops, covering approximately 36% of the territory. The "Green Line," a demilitarized zone maintained by the United Nations Peacekeeping Force in Cyprus (UNFICYP), separates the two parts.

In 1983, the Turkish Cypriot administration in the north declared independence, establishing the Turkish Republic of Northern Cyprus (TRNC).

However, this declaration has only been recognized by Turkey, and the international community considers the territory of the TRNC as part of the Republic of Cyprus.

PRESENT DAY:

Cyprus joined the European Union on May 1, 2004, as part of the largest EU enlargement to date.
The accession represented a significant milestone for Cyprus, offering opportunities for economic development, political integration, and regional cooperation.
Although the island is politically divided, only the Republic of Cyprus, which controls the southern part of the island, is internationally recognized and therefore is the only government that represents Cyprus in the EU. The northern area, self-proclaimed as the Turkish Republic of Northern Cyprus (TRNC), is only recognized by Turkey and is not a member of the EU.
The island is physically divided by the "Green Line," a buffer zone patrolled by the United Nations Peacekeeping Force in Cyprus (UNFICYP). This division separates the Greek Cypriot-majority Republic of Cyprus in the south from the Turkish Cypriot-majority TRNC in the north.
The declaration of independence by the TRNC in 1983 has not been recognized internationally, except by Turkey.
This has been a significant obstacle to international relations and reconciliation on the island.
There have been numerous efforts and rounds of negotiations to reunify the island under a bi-communal and bi-zonal federal framework.
These efforts, facilitated by the UN, have sought to resolve key issues such as security, governance, territory, and property.
However, despite some progress and the willingness to compromise shown at different times by both communities, a lasting solution has not yet been achieved.
Nevertheless, foreigners coming to live on the island do not feel any ongoing conflict, as there has been no type of armed or military aggression for about 50 years.

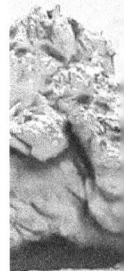

31
CYPRUS BANKING CRISIS.

The Cyprus banking crisis is a significant event in the recent economic history of Europe, occurring in 2012-2013.

This episode was part of the European sovereign debt crisis and had significant consequences for both the economy of Cyprus and the Eurozone as a whole.

Here are the key points of this crisis:

Background

-Real estate bubble and banking expansion: Before the crisis, Cypriot banks experienced significant expansion, partly due to investment in the real estate sector and the acquisition of Greek government bonds.
-Global financial crisis: The 2008 financial crisis negatively affected Cypriot banks, exacerbating problems stemming from their exposure to the over-indebted real estate sector and Greek public debt.

Triggers

-Greek debt haircut: In 2011, as part of the measures to address the debt crisis in Greece, a significant haircut was imposed on Greek government bonds, which severely affected Cypriot banks due to their large exposure to these assets.
-Loss of confidence and capital flight: The financial situation of Cypriot banks deteriorated rapidly, leading to a crisis of confidence among depositors and a flight of capital.

Consequences

- **Financial bailout:** In March 2013, Cyprus reached an agreement with the troika (European Commission, European Central Bank, and International Monetary Fund) for a bailout package of 10 billion euros. This agreement included tough measures such as restructuring banks and imposing losses on uninsured depositors (a process known as "bail-in").
- **Capital controls:** To prevent a massive flight of capital, the Cypriot government imposed capital controls, an unprecedented measure in the eurozone that restricted the free movement of capital.
- **Economic and social impact:** The crisis had a profound impact on the Cypriot economy, leading to a recession, increased unemployment, and the erosion of household wealth.
- **Reforms and recovery:** In exchange for the bailout, Cyprus committed to significant structural reforms. Despite the depth of the crisis, the Cypriot economy began to show signs of recovery in the following years.

Response: Financial and Banking Reforms

- **Restructuring of the banking sector:** The size of the Cypriot banking sector was reduced, and major banks were restructured, including the winding down of Laiki Bank and the transfer of some of its assets and liabilities to the Bank of Cyprus.
- **Strengthening of financial regulation and supervision:** Cyprus strengthened its regulatory and supervisory framework for banking to improve risk management and increase the financial sector's resilience.

Response: Fiscal and Public Administration Reforms

- **Fiscal consolidation:** Cyprus implemented austerity measures to reduce the public deficit, including cuts in public spending and tax increases.
- **Public administration reform:** Reforms were carried out to improve the efficiency of the public sector, including reducing bureaucracy and enhancing digital public services.

Response: Labor market and pension reforms

-Labor market reform: Reforms were introduced to make the labor market more flexible and improve competitiveness, including measures to facilitate hiring and firing.
-Pension system reform: Changes were implemented to ensure the sustainability of the pension system, including raising the retirement age.
-Reforms and policies to attract investors, businesses, and digital nomads: These measures sought not only to recover economic stability but also to diversify the country's economic base and promote sustainable growth.

Some of the most notable initiatives include:

-Citizenship by Investment Scheme: Although it was later suspended in 2020 due to concerns about its integrity and pressure from the European Union, this program allowed foreign investors to obtain Cypriot citizenship in exchange for significant investments in the country.
This included investments in real estate, local businesses, investment funds, or through job creation.
-Tax Incentives: Cyprus has offered a series of tax incentives to attract businesses and professionals:

   1. Competitive corporate tax: With one of the lowest corporate tax rates in the EU (12.5%), Cyprus has positioned itself as an attractive destination for international companies.
   2. Non-domiciled regime: Residents not domiciled in Cyprus, who meet certain criteria, can benefit from exemptions on dividend and interest income, as well as capital gains under certain conditions.
   3. Incentives for innovation and startups: Tax deductions have been introduced for investments in innovation, R&D, and startups.

4. Digital nomad Visa: In response to the growing trend of remote work, Cyprus has launched a visa for digital nomads, allowing remote workers from outside the EU to live in Cyprus while working for employers or clients outside the country. This visa offers an attractive environment due to the climate, quality of life, and tax incentives.

5. Simplification of procedures for businesses: Cyprus has worked on simplifying administrative and registration procedures for new businesses, aiming to reduce bureaucracy and facilitate the start and operation of businesses. This includes improving digital services for business registration and tax management.

6. Development of infrastructure and services: Investment in high-quality infrastructure, such as telecommunications, energy, and transportation, along with the promotion of high-quality financial, legal, and business services, have made Cyprus an attractive destination for international companies.

7. Promotion of the energy and natural gas sector: The exploitation of natural gas fields in Cyprus's Exclusive Economic Zone has opened new opportunities for investors in the energy sector, seeking to turn Cyprus into an energy hub in the Mediterranean.

Results of the recovery

By 2024, Cyprus has achieved a notable economic recovery from the depths of its financial crisis:

-**Economic growth:** The Cypriot economy experienced sustained growth in the years following the crisis, driven by investment, consumption, and growth in sectors such as tourism, energy, and financial services.

-**Reduction of unemployment:** The unemployment rate, which had reached record levels during the crisis, decreased significantly thanks to economic recovery and labor market reforms, reaching 6.4% in 2024.

-**Financial stability:** Cypriot banks have become more stable and resilient, with improved capital and liquidity ratios.

- **End of capital controls:** Cyprus has successfully lifted all capital controls that were imposed during the crisis, restoring confidence in the financial system.
- **Improvement in investor confidence:** The reforms implemented and the economic recovery have helped to restore investor confidence in Cyprus.

32

MOST IMPORTANT CITIES AND TOURIST ATTRACTIONS.

Population census

In 2024, Cyprus has an estimated total population of 875,900 inhabitants.

The population distribution in the 7 most important cities of Cyprus is as follows:

-**Nicosia:** Approximately 330,000 inhabitants. It is the capital and the largest city of Cyprus, acting as the main political, administrative, and cultural center.
-**Limassol:** Has about 240,000 inhabitants. Known for being a major financial center and maritime port.
-**Larnaca:** Home to about 72,000 inhabitants. A coastal city known for its beaches and for hosting Cyprus's main airport.
-**Famagusta:** Has around 42,000 inhabitants. An important tourist destination, although part of its area is in the zone administered by the Turkish Republic of Northern Cyprus.
-**Paphos:** Approximately 35,900 inhabitants. A UNESCO World Heritage site and popular tourist destination.
-**Ayia Napa:** About 2,900 inhabitants live here. Famous for its beaches and vibrant nightlife.

Regarding the foreign community, approximately 22% of the population in Cyprus is foreign, representing about 192,698 individuals.

The estimated distribution of foreigners by nationality, based on migration patterns up to 2024, is as follows:

-**Greeks:** They constitute about 86,714 (45%) of the foreign population, reflecting a close cultural and historical relationship between Greece and Cyprus.

- **British:** Approximately 38,540 (20%) of the total foreigners. Cyprus is a popular destination for British expatriates due to its climate, language (English is widely spoken), and historical ties.
- **Russians:** About 19,270 (10%), attracted by the climate, investment opportunities, and quality of life.
- **Romanians and Bulgarians:** Each group represents around 9,635 (5%) of the foreigners, reflecting labor mobility within the European Union.
- **Others:** Include a variety of nationalities totaling approximately 28,905 (15%) of the total foreigners in Cyprus.

Key characteristics and tourist attractions

1. Nicosia (Lefkosia):

Nicosia, the capital of Cyprus, is a city of deep history and significant commercial activity, marked by its unique position as the last divided capital in the world.

With roots dating back more than 4,500 years, Nicosia has been the administrative, political, cultural, and economic heart of Cyprus since the 10th century.

- **Ancient history and foundation:** Nicosia developed as an important administrative and commercial center in the Bronze Age. Over the centuries, the city has been influenced by numerous civilizations, including Assyrians, Egyptians, Persians, and Romans, due to its strategic location in the Mediterranean.
- **Byzantine and medieval era:** During the Byzantine period, Nicosia served as an important administrative and defensive center. The construction of the Venetian walls in the 16th century, of which three gates and part of the walls are still preserved, was a highlight of its defensive architecture designed to protect the city from invaders.

- **Ottoman and british rule:** Under Ottoman rule, which began in 1571, Nicosia maintained its importance as an administrative center. However, it was during the British administration, starting in 1878, when Nicosia began to modernize significantly, introducing new infrastructure and expanding its commercial role.
- **Division of Nicosia:** The Turkish invasion of 1974 led to the division of Nicosia (and Cyprus), with the creation of the "Green Line" separating the southern part, controlled by Greek Cypriots, from the northern part, administered by Turkish Cypriots. This division has had a profound impact on the city's life and economy.
- **Commercial activity and development:** Today, Nicosia is a thriving center of trade and business. The southern part of the city houses the government of the Republic of Cyprus, as well as numerous embassies, banks, and international corporations.

The service sector, especially financial, legal, and educational services, plays a crucial role in the city's economy.

The city is also a significant retail hub, featuring a mix of traditional bazaars and modern shopping malls. Ledra Street, in the heart of the old city, is a popular shopping and leisure destination.
- **Challenges and future:** Nicosia faces the unique challenge of operating and developing under the shadow of political and territorial division, however, the city continues to strive to be a meeting place for dialogue and cooperation between the Greek Cypriot and Turkish Cypriot communities.

Some tourist attractions:

- **The green line:** This is the demilitarized zone that divides Nicosia in two, separating the southern part controlled by Greek Cypriots from the northern part occupied by Turks. Walking along the Green Line offers a unique perspective on the recent history of Cyprus.
- **The Cyprus archaeological museum:** This is the island's main archaeological museum, where visitors can see artifacts spanning over 8,500 years of Cypriot history, from the Neolithic era to the Roman period.

- **Famagusta gate**: Originally one of the three gates that were part of the Venetian walls surrounding the old city, it now serves as a cultural center for exhibitions and events.
- **Laiki Geitonia district**: Located within the city walls, this restored pedestrian neighborhood is known for its winding streets, souvenir shops, craft workshops, and traditional cafes.
- **St. John's cathedral**: An impressive Orthodox church with beautiful frescoes inside. Although it is small, its rich decoration and historical significance make it a must-visit.
- **Byzantine museum**: Houses one of the richest collections of Byzantine art in Cyprus, including icons, frescoes, and other religious artifacts.
- **Venetian walls**: Built in the 16th century by the Venetians to protect the city from invaders, today, parts of the wall and some of its gates and bastions still stand, offering a glimpse into Nicosia's military past.
- **The house of dragoman hadjigeorgakis kornesios**: One of the best-preserved Ottoman houses and an impressive example of 18th-century urban architecture in Nicosia. It is now a museum showcasing what life was like during the Ottoman period.
- **Armenian quarter and armenian museum**: Explores the history and culture of the Armenian community in Cyprus, which has been part of the island's rich cultural mix for centuries.
- **Ledra street**: A popular shopping and pedestrian street that runs north to south through the center of Nicosia, crossing the Green Line. It offers a wide range of shops, cafes, and vantage points to observe the dynamics of the divided city.

2. Limassol (Lemesos):

Limassol, the second largest city in Cyprus, is known for its vital port, rich cultural history, and vibrant commercial life.

Strategically located on the island's southern coast, Limassol has played a crucial role in the history and economy of Cyprus from ancient times to the present day.

-Ancient history and origins: The earliest settlements in the Limassol region date back to antiquity, with evidence of occupation from the second millennium BC. The city itself has roots that can be traced back to the ancient city-states of Kourion and Amathus, two of the major urban centers in ancient Cyprus. These nearby archaeological sites provide evidence of the region's rich cultural and commercial history.

-Byzantine period and middle ages: During the Byzantine period, Limassol served as an important port and military base. Its significance continued into the Middle Ages, especially under the rule of the Lusignan and the Venetians, due to its strategic maritime position. Limassol Castle, located in the heart of the old city, dates from this period and is said to be the site where Richard the Lionheart married Berengaria of Navarre during the Third Crusade.

-Ottoman and british rule: Under Ottoman rule, which began in the late 16th century, Limassol experienced a period of decline. However, this trend was reversed with the British administration in 1878, which brought about the modernization of infrastructure and revitalization of the port, fostering trade and economic activity.

-Modern development and commercial activity: In the 20th and early 21st centuries, Limassol has transformed into a dynamic business and commerce center. Its port is one of the busiest in the Mediterranean, handling a significant portion of Cyprus's maritime trade and passenger traffic.

The city has also become an important center for the cruise industry. Moreover, Limassol is a financial and services hub, attracting international investments and companies from around the world. The city has seen significant real estate development, with the construction of modern residential complexes, office buildings, and shopping centers.

Events like the Limassol Carnival and Wine Festival attract both local and international visitors, promoting Cypriot culture and traditions.

Some tourist attractions:

- **Limassol castle:** Located in the heart of the old town, this medieval castle houses the Cyprus Medieval Museum. According to legend, it was here that Richard the Lionheart married Berenguela of Navarre.
- **Molos promenade:** A long and beautiful pedestrian area along the coast, perfect for walking, cycling, or just enjoying the sea breeze. It is lined with palm trees, parks, and play areas.
- **Limassol marina:** A modern marina that combines luxury shopping, restaurants, and bars, with an impressive array of yachts and boats. It's an excellent place to enjoy the luxurious atmosphere of Limassol.
- **Fasouri watermania water park:** One of the largest water parks in Cyprus, it offers a variety of water slides, pools, and attractions for all ages. It's a fun option for a family day out.
- **Kourion:** An important archaeological site near Limassol, with impressive ruins that include a well-preserved Greco-Roman theatre, houses with mosaics, and an ancient stadium.
- **Sanctuary of apollo hylates:** Near Kourion, this was one of the main religious centers of ancient Cyprus, dedicated to the god Apollo. The remains include a temple, a portico, and a sacred bath.
- **Cyprus wine museum:** Located in Erimi, near Limassol, it offers visitors the chance to learn about the history of wine on the island, dating back over 5,000 years, and to taste local wines.
- **Kolossi castle:** A castle built in the 13th century by the Knights of St. John, it is a magnificent example of medieval military architecture and a perfect spot for history enthusiasts.
- **Akrotiri salt lake:** An important wetland area that attracts a wide variety of birds, including flamingos during certain times of the year. It is ideal for nature lovers and bird watching.

- **The old town:** The historic heart of Limassol, with its narrow streets, craft shops, traditional cafes, and markets.
It is the perfect place to experience local charm and shop for souvenirs.
- **Limassol municipal market:** A bustling market where visitors can find everything from fresh fruits and vegetables to local products and handicrafts. It's an authentic cultural experience and a great place to sample Cypriot cuisine.

3. Larnaca (Larnaka):

Larnaca, one of the oldest cities in Cyprus, harmoniously combines its rich history with a vibrant modern commercial activity.

Located on the southeastern coast of the island, Larnaca is known for its fascinating mix of cultural influences, the result of thousands of years of history, and its strategic location in the Mediterranean, which has made it an important port and commercial center throughout the centuries.

- **Ancient history:** The area around Larnaca has been inhabited since prehistoric times, as evidenced by archaeological findings in the area. In antiquity, the city was known as Kition, or Citium in English, founded by the Phoenicians in the 13th century BC. Kition was an important commercial and maritime center, thanks to its natural harbor and location on Mediterranean trade routes. The city had strong ties with the Phoenician and Greek world, which is reflected in the archaeological remains that include sanctuaries and fortifications.
- **Byzantine period and middle ages:** Throughout the Byzantine era, Larnaca continued to be an important anchorage and trading center. During the Middle Ages, under the rule of the Lusignan and later the Venetians, Larnaca maintained its importance due to its port, which played a vital role in trade between the East and West.

-Modern era: With the arrival of Ottoman rule in the 16th century, Larnaca became the gateway to Cyprus, welcoming diplomats, merchants, and pilgrims. During the British period, which began in 1878, the city's infrastructure was modernized and its port was expanded, further consolidating its role as a key commercial center.

-Contemporary commercial activity: Today, Larnaca is both a popular tourist destination and a thriving commercial hub. Its airport, Larnaca International Airport, is one of the two main entry points to Cyprus, facilitating both trade and tourism. The city also remains an important port, handling cargo and passengers. Larnaca also benefits from a vibrant commercial scene, with a mix of traditional shops and modern shopping centers offering everything from local crafts to international brands. The city is known for its salt production and has developed sectors in services, education, and real estate.

Some tourist attractions:

-Larnaca salt lake (Alyki): A protected natural area that attracts flamingos and other migratory birds in winter. The lake is also known for the nearby Hala Sultan Tekke mosque, a sacred site for Muslims.

-St. Lazarus church (Agios Lazaros): An impressive 9th-century Orthodox church built over the tomb of Lazarus, the friend of Jesus who, according to tradition, lived in Larnaca after his resurrection. The church is an excellent example of Byzantine architecture in Cyprus.

-Larnaca fort: A medieval castle that serves as a museum and offers spectacular sea views from its walls. It is believed to have been built during the reign of James I of Cyprus (14th century) and has been used as a prison and barracks.

-Finikoudes promenade: One of the most famous beaches in Cyprus, known for its palm trees and its bustling avenue filled with cafes, bars, and restaurants. It's the perfect place to enjoy the Mediterranean sun and Cypriot hospitality.

- **Larnaca district archaeological museum:** Where one can explore artifacts dating from prehistory to the Roman period, providing insight into the rich history of the region.
- **Kamares aqueduct:** An impressive 18th-century aqueduct, known as the Kamares, which was used to transport water to Larnaca from a source 10 km away. Its elegant construction and the row of arches make it a photogenic site.
- **Larnaca port and marina:** A lively place to stroll, with a mix of traditional fishing boats and luxurious yachts. The area also has a good selection of restaurants and cafes.
- **Pierides museum:** Houses one of the oldest private collections in Cyprus, spanning over 4,000 years of the island's history, including artifacts from the Bronze Age, Greco-Roman periods, and Byzantine art.
- **Hala sultan tekke mosque:** Located near Larnaca Salt Lake, this mosque is one of the most sacred Islamic sites outside Saudi Arabia. According to legend, it is the resting place of Umm Haram, aunt of Muhammad.
- **Choirokoitia archaeological area:** Though a bit away from Larnaca, this prehistoric site is one of the most important Neolithic settlements in the eastern Mediterranean and has been declared a UNESCO World Heritage Site.

4. Paphos (Pafos):

Paphos, located on the southwest coast of Cyprus, is a city of great historical and cultural importance as well as a significant tourist center. Its history extends from prehistoric times to the present day, through Hellenistic, Roman, Byzantine, Frankish, Venetian, Ottoman, and British periods.

- **Ancient history and origins:** Paphos is known in Greek mythology as the birthplace of Aphrodite, the goddess of love and beauty, which has attracted visitors to the region since antiquity.
The city was the capital of the kingdom of Cyprus during the Hellenistic and Roman periods, contributing to its wealth and development.

The archaeological site of Nea Paphos is a testament to this golden era, with its stunning mosaics dating from the 3rd century AD, which are considered among the most beautiful in the Mediterranean world.
-**Medieval to modern times:** During the Middle Ages, Paphos lost some of its importance in favor of other cities in Cyprus.
However, it maintained its relevance as an ecclesiastical center. Under Ottoman and later British rule, Paphos slowly transformed but did not regain its former splendor until the 20th century.
-**Commercial activity:** Today, Paphos' economy is primarily centered around tourism. The city offers a wide range of tourist services, including hotels, restaurants, bars, and recreational activities such as golf, diving, and hiking.
Paphos is also known for its port, which serves both as a hub of commercial activity and as a starting point for cruises and sea excursions.
The Paphos Cultural Festival and the Paphos Opera Festival attract both international and local visitors with performances of music, dance, and theater. Additionally, the city was named a European Capital of Culture in 2017, which spurred the renovation of its cultural infrastructure and raised its international profile.

Some tourist sites:

-**Paphos archaeological park:** A vast site that houses impressive ancient ruins, including well-preserved Roman mosaic houses depicting mythological scenes,
the Odeon, and the remains of palaces and tombs.
-**Tombs of the kings:** An impressive necropolis dating from the 4th century BC that covers a vast area.
Despite its name, the site was the resting place of high officials and aristocrats rather than royalty.
-**Paphos castle:** Located at the edge of the harbor, this Byzantine castle was rebuilt by the Lusignans in the 13th century and later fortified by the Ottomans. It offers wonderful views of the harbor and is a popular photographic landmark.
-**Paphos lighthouse:** Near the Archaeological Park, this lighthouse is an ideal spot for enjoying panoramic views of the coast and surrounding landscape.

- **Aphrodite's rock:** According to mythology, this impressive rock rising from the sea is the birthplace of Aphrodite, the Greek goddess of love and beauty. It is located between Paphos and Limassol and is a magnificent place to watch the sunset.
- **Aphrodite's baths:** Located on the Akamas Peninsula, this natural pool is said to be where Aphrodite bathed.

The surrounding area, filled with natural trails, is perfect for hiking and enjoying the local flora and fauna.
- **Panagia chrysopolitissa church:** At this site stands St. Paul's Pillar, where, according to tradition, the apostle was whipped before converting the Roman governor to Christianity.

The remains of a 4th-century basilica can also be explored here.
- **Agios neophytos monastery:** Founded by the monk and hermit Neophytos in the 12th century, this monastery houses impressive Byzantine frescoes and offers a glimpse into monastic life in Cyprus.
- **Paphos forest:** A vast and verdant refuge that offers coolness and a great opportunity for bird watching, especially in the Cedar Valley region, where endemic Cypriot cedars can be seen.
- **Byzantine museum:** Located in the center of Paphos, this museum holds a rich collection of Byzantine icons and other religious artifacts dating from the 9th to the 18th centuries.

5. Ayia Napa:

Ayia Napa, located on the southeast coast of Cyprus, has evolved from a quiet fishing village into one of the island's most popular tourist destinations, known for its beautiful beaches and vibrant nightlife.

Despite its current fame as a leisure and entertainment hub, Ayia Napa also has a rich cultural and religious history.

- **Ancient history and origins:** The name "Ayia Napa" translates to "Holy Napa," derived from an ancient Greek word meaning "sacred forest." According to legend, a hunter discovered an icon of the Virgin Mary in a cave hidden within the forest, giving rise to the place's name and the establishment of the monastery that still stands in the heart of Ayia Napa.

- **Development and growth:** For centuries, Ayia Napa remained a small agricultural and fishing community, relatively isolated due to its location on the eastern tip of Cyprus.
However, its fortunes began to change in the 1970s when Cyprus began to develop its tourism industry.
The stunning white sandy beaches and crystal-clear waters of Ayia Napa made it an attractive destination for tourists.
- **Commercial activity:** The economy of Ayia Napa largely revolves around tourism. The town offers a wide range of activities, from water sports and diving to boat excursions and music events. WaterWorld Aquatic Park, themed after ancient Greece, is one of the largest water parks in Europe and a major family attraction. The area is also known for its diverse culinary offerings, including both traditional Cypriot cuisine and international options. Local markets and shops sell handicrafts, souvenirs, and typical products of the island.

Some tourist sites:

- **Ayia Napa monastery:** Located in the heart of Ayia Napa, this 16th-century monastery is an oasis of peace and tranquility. Built around a cave, the monastery is a beautiful example of medieval architecture and one of the most photographed places in the town.
- **Nissi beach:** Famous for its turquoise waters and fine golden sand, Nissi Beach is one of the most popular beaches in Cyprus. It is a perfect place to enjoy the sun, engage in water sports, and participate in beach parties.
- **Cape greco national forest park:** An area of exceptional natural beauty, ideal for hiking, cycling, and exploring.
The park offers stunning sea views, rock formations, caves, and rich biodiversity.
- **Ayia Napa sea caves:** Located near Cape Greco, these caves are accessible by sea and are a popular spot for diving and swimming. The rock formations and clear waters create a stunning environment for exploration.

- **Thalassa municipal sea museum:** This museum is dedicated to the influence of the sea on the history of Cyprus, displaying everything from ancient artifacts to modern marine fauna. The centerpiece is a replica of an ancient Greek merchant ship.
- **WaterWorld themed waterpark:** One of the largest water parks in Europe, themed around Greek mythology. It offers a wide variety of slides, pools, and water attractions for all ages.
- **Konnos beach:** A beautiful and tranquil beach located between Ayia Napa and Protaras. Surrounded by hills covered in vegetation, it is ideal for those seeking a more relaxed place to swim and sunbathe.
- **Love bridge:** An impressive natural rock formation in the shape of an arch over the sea. It is a popular spot for photography, and according to legend, those who kiss their partner on the bridge will have eternal love.
- **Ayia Napa central square:** The vibrant heart of the town, filled with restaurants, cafes, bars, and shops. During the summer, the square becomes the center of nightlife and entertainment.
- **Potamos Liopetriou:** A picturesque fishing village with traditional houses and colorful boats, ideal for enjoying authentic Cypriot cuisine in a tranquil setting.

6. Famagusta (Ammochostos):

Famagusta, located on the eastern coast of Cyprus, is a city with a rich history that dates back to antiquity.

Throughout the centuries, it has been an important commercial and cultural center, whose significance has fluctuated with the changing dynasties, empires, and cultural influences.

The history of Famagusta is marked by periods of great prosperity and tragic devastations, which have left a legacy of historic monuments and a rich cultural heritage.

- **Origins and antiquity:** It is believed that Famagusta was founded around the 3rd century BC, although the area has been inhabited much earlier. Originally known as Arsinoe, the city thrived under Ptolemaic and then Roman rule, benefiting from its strategic location for maritime trade between the East and the West.
- **Byzantine period:** During the Byzantine period, Famagusta served as an important center of trade and defense. However, the city suffered from attacks and sieges, including Arab invasions that fluctuated its fortune until the arrival of the Crusaders.
- **Medieval flourishing:** The true golden age of Famagusta arrived under the rule of the Lusignan in the 13th century, when it became one of the most important ports in the Mediterranean. The city attracted merchants from around the world, and its wealth was reflected in the construction of magnificent Gothic churches and public buildings. The arrival of the Genoese and later the Venetians continued this era of prosperity, making Famagusta a hub of trade and culture.
- **Venetian and ottoman rule:** Under Venetian rule (from 1489), Famagusta was heavily fortified to protect against the growing Ottoman threats. However, in 1571, after a prolonged siege, the city fell into Ottoman hands. The capture of Famagusta marked the end of Venetian presence in Cyprus and the beginning of a long period of decline for the city, as the center of trade and power shifted to other parts of the empire.
- **Modern era:** After Ottoman rule, Famagusta came under British control in 1878. The city experienced a resurgence as a commercial port, especially after the construction of the railway that connected it to the interior of Cyprus. However, the division of Cyprus in 1974 and the Turkish invasion resulted in the evacuation and abandonment of Varosha, a thriving tourist district of Famagusta, turning it into a ghost town.

-**Current commercial activity:** Today, Famagusta is known for its university and as a center of education. The part of the city under the control of the Turkish Republic of Northern Cyprus has seen development in terms of tourism and education, with the opening of new universities that attract international students. Tourism focuses on the city's rich cultural heritage and its magnificent beaches, although the Varosha district remains inaccessible.

Some tourist sites:

-**Famagusta walls and Othello's tower:** The imposing medieval walls surround the old city of Famagusta, with Othello's Tower, known for having inspired Shakespeare for his play "Othello." The walls and the tower provide a fascinating insight into the military architecture of the time.
-**St. Nicholas cathedral (Lala Mustafa Pasha Mosque):** Originally built as a Gothic cathedral in the 14th century, it now functions as a mosque. It is one of the most impressive examples of Gothic architecture in the Eastern Mediterranean.
-**Bishop's Palace:** Near St. Nicholas Cathedral, the remains of the Bishop's Palace are another testament to the rich history of Famagusta.
-**Church of St. George of the greeks:** Another magnificent example of Gothic architecture, though in ruins, this church still retains its grandeur and is a reminder of Famagusta's importance during the medieval era.
-**St. Barnabas monastery:** Located near Famagusta, this monastery dedicated to St. Barnabas, the patron saint of Cyprus, houses a museum of icons and religious artifacts.
-**Ancient city (Salamis):** A few kilometers north of Famagusta, the ruins of Salamis are one of the most important archaeological sites in Cyprus, featuring a well-preserved theater, gymnasium, and Roman baths.

- **Varosha beach:** Although Varosha, the once popular and now abandoned beach area, is not open to the public, the nearby beaches to Famagusta are some of the most beautiful in Cyprus, offering crystal clear waters and fine sand.
- **Canbulat museum:** Named after the Ottoman commander who played a crucial role in the capture of Famagusta, this museum is located in one of the city gates and showcases the military history of the region.
- **Othello tower:** Part of the medieval fortifications and offers excellent views of the old city and the sea. Although it is often confused with Othello's Bastion, both are worth visiting for their historical significance.
- **Old port:** Although smaller and less active than in its golden era, the port offers a charming promenade, overlooking boats and yachts, surrounded by cafes and restaurants where you can enjoy local cuisine.

33
TYPICAL FOOD

The typical food of Cyprus reflects the rich cultural history and culinary influences the island has received over the centuries, combining elements from Greek, Turkish, and Middle Eastern cuisines.

Here are some of the typical dishes:

-**Meze**: Similar to Spanish tapas, the Cypriot meze is a series of small dishes served together, offering a wide variety of flavors. It can include everything from olives, tahini, tzatziki, and hummus to meat and fish dishes.
-**Souvla**: Large chunks of meat (often lamb, pork, or chicken) grilled on a long skewer. It is a popular dish at family gatherings and festivities.
-**Halloumi**: A semi-hard, salty cheese that can be fried or grilled without melting, thanks to its high melting point.
It originates from Cyprus and is often served with grilled vegetables or as part of a meze.
-**Sheftalia**: Grilled sausages wrapped in a fat net, typically made from pork or lamb, and seasoned with onion, parsley, and spices.
-**Moussaka**: Although it is a dish known in various Balkan and Middle Eastern cuisines, the Cypriot version often includes layers of minced meat and eggplant, topped with a béchamel sauce and baked.
-**Kleftiko**: Lamb cooked slowly in its own juices until it falls apart, traditionally prepared in a sealed clay oven.
It is marinated with garlic, lemon, and herbs before cooking.
-**Koupepia**: Also known as dolmas in other regions, these are vine leaves stuffed with a mix of meat and rice, cooked in a tomato sauce.

- **Loukoumades:** A dessert consisting of small balls of dough fried until they are crispy on the outside and fluffy on the inside, then soaked in honey or syrup and sprinkled with cinnamon and sometimes crushed nuts.
- **Louvi:** A simple but nutritious dish made with black-eyed beans and Swiss chard, often served with chopped onion and olive oil.
- **Afelia:** Pieces of pork marinated in red wine and seasoned with coriander before being cooked. It is a traditional dish often served with potatoes or bulgur.

- **Tzatziki:** Although common in various Eastern Mediterranean cuisines, in Cyprus, this thick yogurt sauce with cucumber, garlic, olive oil, and sometimes mint, is a frequent accompaniment to many meals, especially with meats.
- **Makaronia tou fournou:** Also known as pastitsio in Greece, this is a baked pasta dish that includes layers of macaroni, minced meat, and a creamy béchamel topping.
- **Tarhana:** A thick and nutritious soup made with fermented grains and yogurt, often enriched with vegetables and pieces of meat.
- **Fasolada:** A white bean soup considered the national dish of Cyprus, rich in vegetables and flavored with bay leaves and olive oil.

- **Elioti:** An olive bread, often seasoned with onion and herbs. It is commonly found in bakeries and is perfect to accompany meze.
- **Flaounes:** Baked pastries that are typical at Easter, made with a bread-like dough filled with cheese, eggs, and mint, sometimes adding raisins.
- **Loukaniko:** Cypriot sausage, seasoned with wine and often with coriander seeds and orange, which can be served either fresh or cured.

- **Trachanas:** A soup or porridge dish made from crushed and fermented grains mixed with yogurt or fermented milk, often served hot with pieces of halloumi or kielbasa.
- **Glyko tou koutaliou:** A type of sweet preserve made with whole fruits or nuts, slowly cooked in syrup until caramelized. It is served in small portions, as a gesture of hospitality, accompanied by cold water or coffee.

34

FUN FACTS

-Island of cats: One of the more peculiar facts about Cyprus is that it has a large population of cats. It is said that these animals were brought to the island by Saint Helen in the 4th century to control the snake population. Cats are highly respected and beloved on the island, and you can find many sanctuaries and people who care for them. Additionally, there is a breed known as the Cypriot cat or the "Aphrodite Giant." These cats are large, with muscular bodies and a friendly disposition, and are believed to have been on the island since ancient times.

-Halloumi culture: Cyprus is famous for its halloumi cheese, known worldwide. This cheese has a high melting point, which makes it ideal for frying or grilling. Halloumi is a central element in Cypriot cuisine and has been the subject of "cultural wars" over the designation of origin between Cyprus and other countries.

-The legend of Aphrodite: According to Greek mythology, Aphrodite, the goddess of love and beauty, was born in Cyprus. The specific place associated with her birth is Aphrodite's Rock, near Paphos, a site popular with both tourists and mythology enthusiasts. Visitors often stop their cars nearby to pick up a stone as a souvenir or swim around the rock to find eternal love.

-Commandaria wine: Cyprus is home to Commandaria wine, which is considered one of the oldest wines in the world that is still produced. It is said to have been made in the same way for over 4000 years. This sweet wine was first documented during the Crusades, who called it "the wine of kings."

- **Religious relics:** Cyprus holds a special place in Christianity due to its connections with Saint Paul, who visited the island with Saint Barnabas. Local legend has it that Saint Paul was beaten in Paphos, which left him scarred. Additionally, it is believed that the "Pillar of Saint Paul" in Paphos is where he was tied and whipped.

- **Unique biodiversity:** The island is a crucial stopover for millions of migratory birds. Cyprus is on a major migratory route, and about 15% of Europe's birds pass through the island each year on their way between Europe and Africa.

- **Endemic flora:** Cyprus is home to over 125 plant species found nowhere else in the world. The island is especially known for its endemic orchid species, making it a place of great interest for botanists and nature lovers.

- **World's first democracy:** It is believed that the ancient city-state of Salamis in Cyprus was one of the first to practice some form of democracy, even before ancient Greece. This fact underscores Cyprus's historical significance as a center of cultural and political activity in the ancient Mediterranean.

- **Sport and passion:** Football is the most popular sport in Cyprus, with intense rivalry between major clubs. Matches between teams like APOEL FC and Omonia Nicosia draw large crowds and showcase the sporting fervor of the Cypriots.

- **Coffee culture:** Coffee is an essential part of social life in Cyprus. Cypriot coffee is brewed in a small copper pot and served with a thick sediment. Having coffee in Cyprus often involves long conversations and the opportunity to relax with friends and family.

- **Mount Olympus:** The highest point in Cyprus is Mount Olympus, located in the Troodos mountain range.
It is not only a popular tourist destination for skiing during the winter months but also an excellent place for hiking and enjoying nature throughout the rest of the year.

- **The Kyrenia cup:** One of the most intriguing artifacts discovered in Cyprus is the Kyrenia Cup, a 4th-century BC piece of pottery that changes color when wine instead of water is poured into it, due to its chemical properties.

- **The Wishing tree:** At the Ayia Napa monastery, there is an ancient fig tree known as the "wishing tree." Visitors often tie pieces of cloth or paper with their wishes written on them to the tree's branches, hoping they will come true.

- **Larnaca salt:** The Larnaca Salt Lake is famous not only for its natural beauty but also as an important habitat for migratory birds, including flamingos that stop here in the winter. During the summer, the lake dries up and the salt can be harvested, a practice that has been part of the local economy for centuries.

- **Zallogou water:** There is a unique tradition in Cyprus related to the baptism ceremony called "Zallogou Water."
During this ceremony, the godparent throws coins into the water where the child will be baptized to bring good fortune and prosperity.

- **Rock-cut churches:** In the mountains of Cyprus, several churches and chapels carved directly into the rock can be found, some of which date back to the early days of Christianity. These places are not only spiritual but also impressive works of architectural art.

- **Olive cultivation:** Cyprus has a long history of olive cultivation, with some trees being over a thousand years old. Cypriot olive oil is highly valued for its quality and is an essential ingredient in many local dishes.

- **Love bridge:** In Ayia Napa, there is a natural rock formation known as the Love Bridge. According to local legend, those who kiss their partner while standing on the bridge will be blessed with eternal love. It is a popular spot for both tourists and locals.

- **Flower festival:** In May, Cyprus celebrates the Flower Festival, an event that marks the arrival of spring.
During this festival, cities and towns are filled with parades, music, and, of course, flowers everywhere, with residents displaying elaborate floral arrangements.

- **The enigma of Amathus:** Amathus is one of the oldest archaeological sites in Cyprus, with remains dating back to 1100 BC. It was one of the ancient city-states of Cyprus, and legend has it that it was founded by one of the sons of Heracles.

- **St. Lazarus church:** In Larnaca, you can find the impressive St. Lazarus Church, a magnificent example of Byzantine architecture built in the 9th century. According to tradition, Lazarus of Bethany, whom Jesus raised from the dead, became the Bishop of Larnaca and is believed to be buried here.

- **Cedar forest:** Cyprus is home to a cedar forest in the Troodos region, which is less well-known than the famous cedar forests of Lebanon, but equally impressive. This forest offers spectacular scenery and is an excellent spot for hiking and enjoying nature.

If you have found this book, which details all the processes for creating your company in Cyprus and residing in this country to optimize taxes and improve your quality of life, to be useful and enlightening, we invite you to share your impressions by leaving a review on Amazon.

We greatly value your opinion, as it is crucial for us and for other entrepreneurs seeking reliable and practical information on how to establish themselves in Cyprus to take advantage of its favorable tax regime.

We understand that writing a review might seem like a laborious process, but we ask you to take a few minutes to express your thoughts and experiences.

Your feedback not only helps us improve but also assists others in their entrepreneurial endeavors.

We deeply appreciate your support.

If you want to create your company in Cyprus or need personalized advice to fully understand your tax situation, contact us via:

-Our website: **www.solucionfiscalchipre.com**
-Email: **cyprustaxsolution@gmail.com**
-Mobile phone with WhatsApp: **+357 99953934**

We hope that optimizing your taxes becomes a tangible and effective reality!

www.ingramcontent.com/pod-product-compliance
Lightning Source LLC
Chambersburg PA
CBHW070301230526
45470CB00002B/673